James E. White

the price tags of life

the price tags of life

C. ROY ANGELL

BROADMAN PRESS
Nashville, Tennessee

Library of Congress catalog card number: 59–9692

Printed in the United States of America

10.F59K.S.P.

Contents

the price tags of life

Again, the kingdom of heaven is like unto a merchant man, seeking goodly pearls: who, when he had found one pearl of great price, went and sold all that he had, and bought it.

Again, the kingdom of heaven is like unto a net, that was cast into the sea, and gathered of every kind: which, when it was full, they drew to shore, and sat down, and gathered the good into vessels, but cast the bad away. So shall it be at the end of the world: the angels shall come forth, and sever the wicked from among the just, and shall cast them into the furnace of fire: there shall be wailing and gnashing of teeth.

MATTHEW 13:45–50

1

The Price Tags of Life

Some time ago Fred Smith, executive vice-president of the Gruen Watch Company, spoke at the morning service in our church. His opening sentence startled me and set my mind to working. He had very slowly and earnestly spoken this great truth: "The good things of life have to be paid for in advance while the evil things we do are paid for, generally, on the instalment plan." Immediately I thought of some of the great tragedies of the Old Testament and the price those men paid for the evil they did; then the two parables that Jesus so beautifully told in the thirteenth chapter of Matthew in which he illustrates the price we must pay for some of the good things. In one of them a man discovered in a field where he was working a tremendous treasure, "and for joy thereof goeth and selleth all that he hath, and buyeth that field." Immediately following this parable Jesus told of a man who found a pearl of great price and went and sold all that he had and bought it. From there it was just a step to an interesting incident in the Master's life.

A rich, lovable, handsome young man watching Jesus as he laid his hands on the little children and blessed them, and seeing the kind and gentle spirit in the countenance of the

Master, came running after Jesus as he started to walk away and knelt at his feet. "Good Master," he said, "what must I do to inherit eternal life?" He, too, was looking at something that was most desirable and good, and he sincerely wanted it. But when the Master told him the price, he went away sorrowfully. It was just as Mr. Smith said—"There is a price tag on everything." The old world is a storekeeper. We must pay for what we get. Jesus referred to life as a market place where we go to buy something which we want. If it is something good, we pay for it in advance. If it is something evil, we pay for it on the instalment plan.

Look first at the price we pay for the evil we do. David found a huge price tag on a crime he had committed, and God let him pay. When the first instalment was due, Nathan stood before him and told him a story of a rich man taking the ewe lamb that belonged to a poor man. David, deeply stirred, thundered at Nathan, "Show me the man, and I shall punish him." Nathan pointed his finger at the heart of David and answered with those scorching words, "Thou art the man." David's countenance fell. I am sure he trembled and, like the Pharisee in one of Jesus' stories, slunk away. Only David knows the suffering that followed.

Then another instalment was due. This time Absalom, David's favorite son, had Ammon, his half-brother, killed. With a breaking heart, David let Absalom stay in exile and for three years grieved for him. Then another instalment fell due. A loyal servant of David excitedly related how Absalom, back from exile, was being crowned king and was about to march on the palace. David fled in the night. In his flight one of his old servants, disgusted with him, threw dirt on David and cursed him.

Not long after the battle was over between Absalom's forces

and David's, a runner came to tell David that Absalom was buried under a pile of rocks, with his body full of spears and arrows. Another instalment had come due. The story goes on and on and in a terrible way illustrates the truth that the evil things that we do have price tags on them, and we pay for every one of them.

Sometimes the instalments come close together. Haman, the chief prince of Ahasuerus, became very indignant because Mordecai, a gatekeeper, wouldn't do him obeisance by bowing down when he passed. So he planned to put all of the Jewish people in the kingdom to death and to have a special hanging for Mordecai in the back yard of his palace. He built a scaffold seventy-five feet high. Then the first instalment of his wickedness fell due. The king discovered that Mordecai had saved his life, and ordered Haman to dress Mordecai in the royal robes, put the crown on his head, the royal scepter in his hand, mount him on the king's white charger, and personally to lead the horse through the principal streets of the city with a herald preceding them, proclaiming that this is the man the king would honor above all others in the kingdom. The next instalment came due quickly. The king, discovering Haman's plot, ordered him hanged on the scaffold that he had built for Mordecai.

Sometimes the price tag is not so dramatically portrayed. Sometimes the suffering is never known to the rest of the world, but the still, small voice of our conscience whips us, flays us, and burns us until we cry with Cain of old, "My punishment is greater than I can bear."

Recently at the convention of mayors of the cities of the nation, which met at Miami Beach, they elected a mayor of the United States. This, of course, is the coveted honor, and in his acceptance speech televised across the nation he used a

5

story which was meant to be humorous. It did get a smattering of laughter, but it carried with it this great truth of the suffering that can come to a man through his conscience. In substance he said: "Recently the collector of internal revenue received a check for $5,000 and a brief note from a businessman. It read: 'Please find enclosed $5,000 that I owe on my past income tax. I am sending it to you because I haven't been able to sleep. If I can't sleep now, I will send you the balance of it.' "

Secondly, look at the price tag on the good things in life. This, of course, is what Jesus was talking about primarily when he told the parables of the treasure hidden in the field and the goodly pearl. Both of these stories emphasize the fact that the men sold *all* they had. The price tag on the hidden treasure was everything he owned. The price tag on the goodly pearl was all the pearls he had. In many other places both Jesus and the writers of the New Testament emphasized over and over again that the price of the kingdom of God and eternal life is that we lay at the feet of Jesus *all* that we have. The rich young ruler must sell *all* and give it to the poor if he was to come and follow Jesus. Jesus gathered up the truth one day in a never-to-be-forgotten sentence, "Thou shalt love the Lord thy God with all thy heart, and with all thy soul, and with all thy mind" (Matt. 22:37).

At another time two of the disciples wanted to sit one on the right and one on the left of Jesus when he came into his kingdom. Do you remember his answer? "Ye know not what ye ask. Are ye able to drink of the cup that I shall drink of, and be baptized with the baptism that I am baptized with?" (Matt. 20:22). In other words, Jesus is asking them if they could pay the price for the thing they wanted. It thrills us when they proved it with their lives. According to tradition,

6

every one of them died the death of a martyr for the sake of the kingdom of God. Did you ever stop to think why you elected the fine men who are deacons in your church and the consecrated workers who occupy places of honor and responsibility? Before you selected them, you examined carefully their lives and their habits. You found they were Christians of the first magnitude. You were convinced that they would never do anything that would bring dishonor to your church. You found that their lives adorned the gospel of Jesus Christ. They were good men and women, they belonged to God, they were deeply dedicated. How long did it take them to earn your confidence? It took them years of right living, years of refusing to do things that were evil, years of sacrifice that they might help others, years of faithful stewardship. So the good things have to be paid for in advance.

Bishop Arthur Moore, of the Methodist Church, held a revival in the First Methodist Church in Baton Rouge during my pastorate in that city. He told of this incident from his own life. "I was preaching in a revival in a city not far away, and I noticed that on the back seat at each service was one of the most miserable-looking men I ever saw. He never opened a hymnbook or took any part in the service. He slipped down in the seat till his chin rested on his chest, with unhappiness written all over his face. During one of the services I asked the pastor, in a whisper, what was his trouble. He answered, 'It's a good story. You ask *him* that question.' "

The bishop said: "I slipped around to the door while the benediction was being said and stopped the man as he was hurrying out. In a gentle voice I asked him, 'Why are you so miserable? Won't you tell me what's the matter?' He answered about like this: 'Bishop, I want to be a Christian worse than anything in the world almost, but here's my trouble. I was

7

brought up in Chicago, sleeping in boxcars and empty sheds, half frozen most of the time, hungry about all of the time, while on the lake beautiful yachts lay anchored. And the rich people living in them threw overboard scraps that made me drool. Sometimes I got so mad I couldn't see, and I vowed that one day when I grew up I was going to anchor my own yacht out there, and it was going to be the biggest yacht on the lake. Today I am in a position to make that dream come true, or I will be in a few weeks. I am a rich man, and I own two big farms in Kansas. When the crops are harvested, I am going to sell them and the farms and buy that yacht.'

"The man seemed to have finished his story, and I looked at him and finally asked, 'Well, what has that to do with your being a Christian?' With surprise written all over his face, he said: 'Don't you see, if I surrender my life to God, he might want me to sell those farms and crops and give the money to missions. Wouldn't he?'" Bishop Moore said: "It was my turn to be surprised, and I finally said, 'He might or he might not, but, anyway, you ought not to accept his salvation and redemption until you are willing to give God all that you are and all that you have, if he wants it.' A few days later, when the invitation hymn was being sung, he walked down the aisle with firm steps and knelt at the altar. I knelt by him. His prayer was perfect, 'Dear Lord, you can have the farms and the crops, you can have everything I own, and you can have me if you will forgive my sins and give me peace in my heart.'

"In the services after that he sat near the front, peace and joy in his countenance as he sang the hymns at the top of his voice. On the last day a Western Union telegraph boy brought him a telegram and handed it to him on the porch of the church. As he read it, he just said, 'Humph!' I asked him if it was bad news, and he handed me the telegram. It was from the manager of his farms in Kansas, and it read: 'Millions of grasshoppers out here. We have kept them off with fires and drums and tin pans. Come immediately and take charge. I won't accept further responsibility.' I said to him, 'Are you going?' He answered, 'No.' I asked, 'Why not?' 'I gave those farms and those crops to the Lord. They belong to him. The grasshoppers belong to him, too. If he wants to pasture his grasshoppers on his corn and wheat, that's all right with me.'" The Bishop said: "I stood with my mouth open in astonishment. I didn't quite agree with his practical theology, but his surrender to God was perfect. All that he had he gave. It reminds me of what Jesus said about the woman who bathed his feet with ointment, 'She hath done what she could.'"

There is another thing that I am sure we will never forget, and that is the price that God paid to give us this glorious plan of salvation. It cost God the suffering of his own Son. Jesus paid in advance for the forgiveness of our sins. He paid a terrible price—back lashed to ribbons by a cat-o'-nine-tails, a crown of briers pressed down on his head, big dull spikes driven into quivering hands and feet, long hours of agony before a jeering crowd. How can anyone refuse the redemption he offers?

Again, if we are going to help Christ build the kingdom, we can do it only through helping others. That, too, has a price tag on it. Four young men were standing on a college campus when a dilapidated, paintless old Ford rattled up in a cloud of dust. One of the boys had been watching it intently. He broke from the crowd suddenly, jumped on the running board of the Ford, threw both arms around the old man who was driving it, and hugged him affectionately. He

9

called his classmates and introduced them to his father. A sack of apples and some other things were in the back seat, and after a visit of an hour or two the Ford rattled away, back to the farm. One of the boys jokingly, not maliciously, said: "That's a dilapidated old Ford your father is driving. Do you reckon he will make it back to the farm?" The son answered a little huskily: "I love every rattle in that old Ford. My father is sending me to college with the money he might have used to buy a Cadillac."

Why would a father make such a sacrifice? What is the key to understanding such unselfishness? There is one word and only one word which will explain it. That word lies at the very center of Christianity. John made the power of it live forever when he wrote, "For God so loved the world, that he gave his only begotten Son, that whosoever believeth in him should not perish, but have everlasting life" (John 3:16).

Dear Lord, may we never forget for a single moment the price that Jesus paid for our salvation. Amen.

Ask, and it shall be given you; seek, and ye shall find; knock, and it shall be opened unto you: for every one that asketh receiveth; and he that seeketh findeth; and to him that knocketh it shall be opened.

MATTHEW 7:7–8

Offer unto God thanksgiving; and pay thy vows unto the most High: and call upon me in the day of trouble: I will deliver thee, and thou shalt glorify me.

PSALM 50:14–15

2

The Key to the Vaults

Recently I read an old Scottish legend called "The Key to the Vaults." A shepherd boy tending his sheep on the mountainside saw a strange flower, one that he had never seen before in his Scottish heath. He sat down by it to examine it more closely, then dug it up, root and all. It was so beautiful that he lovingly cupped it in his hands. As he did, the great rock mountain in front of him rolled back its doors as if they were on oiled hinges, and there opened before him the vaults of the mountain. The sun shone in on untold riches—beautiful diamonds, sapphires, rubies, and gold. Awed and astonished, slowly step by step he entered. There was wealth everywhere. He laid down the flower and picked up both arms full of the gold and precious stones. Finally, as he turned to go, a voice quietly warned him, "Don't forget the best, don't forget the best." He stopped and looked around on the piles of jewels and wondered if the things he had chosen were the best; he lingered awhile, searching the treasure hoard with his eyes. Then again he took a step toward the opening, and once more the voice said, "Don't forget the best." He hesitated a moment, then walked out into the sunlight. The great rock doors rolled shut behind him, and sud-

13

denly in his hands there was nothing but dirt. And the voice said, "The key, the beautiful flower, is locked up in the vault."

With this legend in mind, read a few lines from the Sermon on the Mount and one sentence from a psalm. "Ask, and it shall be given you; seek, and ye shall find; knock, and it shall be opened unto you" (Matt. 7:7). "Call upon me in the day of trouble: I will deliver thee" (Psalm 50:15).

The key to the vaults of God's bank is the prayer of a fully surrendered life. "Ask, and ye shall receive." "Call upon me in your need; in your hour of trouble, I will deliver." This great truth runs through the Bible from Genesis to Revelation. It is like the vein of gold-bearing quartz, called the mother lode, that runs the length of the Sierra Nevada Mountains and comes to the surface ever and anon. It brings to mind the comforting verse, "Jesus Christ the same yesterday, and to day, and for ever."

Look closely at these two statements. To whom were they spoken? Is God saying to everybody in the world, "Ask, and it shall be given you," and, "Call upon me . . . I will deliver thee"? Is he making these wholesale promises to people who defy him and to people who do not know him? Can just anyone lift these two sentences out of their context and use them as certified checks in God's bank? The answer is no. Each statement is conditioned. Preceding each one God has written down similar requirements.

Open your New Testament to the Sermon on the Mount and look carefully at the order in which these two statements of Jesus come. Just a few lines separate "Ask, and ye shall receive" from the plea that Jesus made, "Seek ye first the kingdom of God . . . and all these things shall be added unto you." And the plea of Jesus comes first. The most wel-

14

come prayer that ever goes up to heaven is the prayer of a penitent soul. It may be in the words of the publican, "God, be merciful to me, a sinner," or it may be a stuttering, stammering voice of a man asking for forgiveness of his sins. However inarticulate he may be, if he is asking Christ to come take over his life, that prayer will be heard and answered. Then, and only then, can he "ask any thing in my name" and have the assurance that it will be given. The key to the vaults of God belongs to him then.

Then, open your Old Testament to Psalm 50 and look closely. "Call upon me . . . I will deliver thee" is not the complete sentence, although it is recorded as a separate verse. The first word in the fifteenth verse is the conjunction *and*. The complete sentence reads, "Offer unto God thanksgiving; and pay thy vows unto the most High: and call upon me in the day of trouble: I will deliver thee, and thou shalt glorify me." So we cannot lift it out of its context and use it as a certified check to just anyone in the world. It is conditioned on two pleas from our Heavenly Father.

First, "offer unto God thanksgiving." Another translation of that clause reads, "Make thanksgiving your offering." This seems to fit better into the context, for God has just said: "If I were hungry, I would not tell thee: for the world is mine, and the fulness thereof. Will I eat the flesh of bulls, or drink the blood of goats?" Of course not. God's hunger is satisfied by our love and loyalty and gratitude. Close by this passage is another that reads, "Come into my courts with thanksgiving." Do we always go up to God's house to worship with a humble and a contrite heart and a spirit of thanksgiving? Or do we sometimes come up fretting and a little rebellious? Do we come out of duty and because we are a little afraid that something might happen to us if we stayed away?

15

There is no way really to worship God unless there is sincere gratitude in our hearts. We worship him in spirit only when we are deeply conscious of the great debt we owe him for all the blessings of life. When we have a heart full of gratitude, it will be easy to express it and it will make the hard places in the road of life so much smoother.

Dr. Howard Kelly, one of the great Christian physicians of Baltimore, related to me a most interesting illustration of this glorious truth. "In my hospital I had a nurse in training who was a lovely young lady, beautiful of face, pure in heart. She was a happy Christian who adorned the gospel of Christ. Every patient that came under her care loved her dearly. Not only the patients but one of the finest young doctors who was interning fell deeply in love with her. They planned to be married when she finished her training. They say, 'Everybody loves a lover,' and everybody loved these two and smiled when they saw them standing close together in the corridor, whispering to each other with the love light shining in their faces. They were married just after she was graduated.

"A little over a year they lived in complete contentment. Then one day they brought the young doctor into the hospital with an incurable disease. It broke the hearts of all of us. She nursed him lovingly until the Lord took him home. About a month later she came back to work on our staff. I dodged her. They had been in my home to dinner, and I felt very close to them. I just didn't want to meet her. I knew that anything I tried to say to comfort her would do no good. I stayed away from her but suffered with her.

"Of course, it was inevitable that I should come face to face with her. When I did, she slipped her arm through mine and said, 'You've been dodging me.' I said, 'Yes, I have. I didn't know what to say. I couldn't think of anything to say that

16

would help heal your broken heart.' To my utter amazement, she just stood there smiling. Then she said, 'Dr. Kelly, I have no bitterness in my heart. I am very grateful to God. God gave me more than he gave any other woman. He gave me two years, two beautiful years—the one before we were married and the one after we were married. I had the love of the finest man that ever lived for two whole years, enough to last me a lifetime. Dr. Kelly, you are all wrong. You don't need to say a word. I say a prayer of thanksgiving every day.' "

It takes a great soul to have an attitude like that. The reverse of it is true. A perennial attitude of thankfulness will build a great soul. The writer of the psalm said, "Make thanksgiving your sacrifice." He is implying that it costs something to be thankful, and it does. It is so much easier to be rebellious. It is so much easier to be sullen and angry. It is so much easier to swell up with self-pity. Being thankful is sometimes a sacrifice that is costly. When it is, then God enters it on the credit side of the ledger in his bank. Maybe this is why it is written down first in the sentence that contains his invitation to us, "Call, and he will deliver us."

The second plea is, "And pay thy vows unto the most High." Fulfil thy commitments. Do the things that you promised God when you accepted his forgiveness, his mercy, and his salvation. Maybe through the years as you have run into difficulties you have made some commitment or some pledge. Maybe you promised him something in a quiet hour of deep consecration when you drew close to God and God drew close to you. Did you keep those promises to God? Did you pay those vows?

There was a deacon in one of my former churches whose first name was Walter. He was one of the finest, one of the

17

best. In the years that we worked together I never asked Walter to do something that he didn't readily, without any hedging, say, "I'll do it if I can." One day we needed a man to be chairman of a campaign. Four men refused or made excuses. I was reluctant to ask Walter, for he already was overworked, but we needed a big man and he was big. I sat down by his desk and outlined the need to him. Back came the same answer: "I'll do it if I can, Brother Roy. I'll do it if I can." Then eagerly he said, "Tell me all about it." "Walter, you tell me something first," I said, "one thing I'd like to know about you. You never have in your life refused to do anything I've wanted you to do. What happened to make you like that?"

He said, "Something happened all right to make me like that. One day that little girl, for whom you performed a wedding ceremony recently, was very ill. It was when she was twelve years old. The doctor walked out of her sickroom one night and said, 'Walter, we've done all we can do. She's in the hands of God. Her temperature is nearly one hundred and five.' After a moment he asked, 'Walter, can you pray?' And I said: 'Yes, sir. Yes, sir. I have some credit [and I'm using his words], I have some credit up there.' 'Well, Walter, if you can pray, go pray.' My wife and I went out on the back porch steps and sat down. We thanked God for our little girl. We thanked him for the happiness and joy that this, our only child, had brought us in these twelve years. We told him that there would be no resentment in our hearts if he took her. Then I added, 'But God, if you'll let us keep her, you can call on me for anything in this world, and I'll do it.' " He said: "Roy, I know you can't bargain with God, and I wasn't trying to, but I was promising him something. So I'm just keeping my commitments, and I get a lot of pleasure out of it."

18

Pay your vows; keep your commitments to God. You promised him something, didn't you? Suppose for a moment that you came face to face with some great trial like the one that Walter faced? How would you begin your prayer? Would you have to say: "Lord, I have no right to ask you for anything. You know my life is wicked; you know I don't go to church; you know I don't ever talk to you except when I need something or I'm in trouble." Would you have to preface your petition like that? Or could you lift your face to heaven and say, "Lord, I need a little extra help," and have the grand assurance that your prayer was heard and that all things would work together for good for you?

All of it could be summed up in Psalm 91:1, 15: "He that dwelleth in the secret place of the most High shall abide under the shadow of the Almighty." "He shall call upon me, and I will answer him: I will be with him in trouble; I will deliver him, and honour him."

Dear Lord, may we be so thankful and so faithful that we can use the key to thy vaults whenever we need a little extra help. Amen.

> *Come unto me, all ye that labour and are heavy laden, and I will give you rest. Take my yoke upon you, and learn of me; for I am meek and lowly in heart: and ye shall find rest unto your souls. For my yoke is easy, and my burden is light.*

MATTHEW 11:28–30

3

Electives of Life

In the foyer of Johns Hopkins University, facing the entrance, stands a marble statue of Jesus. It portrays him leaning forward, arms outstretched as though he were reaching for some wounded, staggering sufferer. On the base of the statue are the words, "Come unto me, all ye that labour and are heavy laden, and I will give you rest." These words have been the text of innumerable sermons. At some time in life all of us belong to the crowd who "labour and are heavy laden." Maybe this is the most appealing invitation Jesus ever gave. It has a rightful place in the center of our thinking and our preaching.

Likewise, the last clause, "My yoke is easy, and my burden is light," states one of the biggest messages of Christianity. The yoke of Jesus is so easy in comparison with the yoke that sin lays on us. Read again the words of Cain, the world's first murderer: "My burden is heavier than I can bear." As I write these words, there is a man in the hospital who wants to die. He has stayed drunk for years. His home fell to pieces. His family disowned him. I asked him why he started to drink, and he said, "To drown my troubles." His burden was heavier than he could bear. Yes, this sentence has a place, too, among the choice sayings of Jesus.

There is one other part of this verse that has been sadly neglected. It contains a thought, while not as attractive as the other two, that is as vital to our well-being and happiness here on earth as anything Jesus ever said. It reads, "Learn of me." It pictures Jesus as a teacher. There are some things that we can learn only from Jesus. If we are to live life at its best, we need to enrol in this university of life and sit at the feet of the great Teacher. As in every institution of learning, there are some *required* courses and some *elective* courses. So in this world university we learn from Jesus that there are some things in which we have no choice, while in others we are free agents.

Look briefly at the *required* courses in this university of life. The <u>first</u> one is life itself. We did not choose to be born; we were not consulted about living at all; but now that we are here, there isn't anything we can do to stop living. We have to live. It is required. There is no escaping. Someone may say, "I can destroy myself, or I can take my own life." The answer, of course, is that you can destroy your body and the temple in which you live. You can wreck it, and it will go back "earth to earth, ashes to ashes, and dust to dust," but *you* will keep on living. Life doesn't end at death. Jesus proved it in his resurrection. His teachings are full of it. This is one of the things that Jesus wanted us to "learn of me." Live you must; it's a required course.

The <u>second</u> among these required courses is death. There will come a time when each of us will walk down the "valley of the shadow." One day our long-distance call will come, and we will "shuffle off this mortal coil." We may as well smile about it as cry. We cannot change it. We can't bypass death. It, too, is a required course. Somewhere in God's infinite wisdom he saw that it would not be good for man to live on earth always. We need to learn from Jesus, as he talked to all of us in the fourteenth chapter of John, that death is not a catastrophe but oftentimes it is a glorious blessing. Paul thought of it as his coronation day when he said: "The time of my departure is at hand. I have fought a good fight, I have finished my course, . . . henceforth there is laid up for me a crown of righteousness" (2 Tim. 4:6–8).

The third required course in this school of life is the judgment bar of God. "It is appointed unto men once to die, but after this the judgment" (Heb. 9:27). Jesus made this very plain as he taught in the university of life. One day we shall stand before the great Judge, and everyone shall give an account of himself. We may cover things up here, we may hide them and conceal them from the eyes of others; but there is coming a time when the book of life will be opened and our records will be made bare. The searching eyes of God miss nothing. This great truth should make us very still and, oh, so careful how we live.

But I turn quickly and joyfully to the *electives* in this university of life. There are many of them, but look closely at three which surely are among the most important.

First, you can choose your way of life. Jesus drew us a picture of this when he said, "Strait is the gate, and narrow is the way, which leadeth unto life . . . wide is the gate, and broad is the way, that leadeth to destruction" (Matt. 7:13–14). God will not use his power to thrust us through either of these gates. It is your choice, as the poet said:

> "But to every man there openeth
> A High Way, and a Low,
> And every man decideth
> The Way his soul shall go."

Russell Conwell used an incident from his life to make this great truth live. "My father bought a farm in New England, and we all went up to build a new home on it. The site my father selected was close to the river in a beautiful piece of bottom land. Hardly had he started with the foundation when some of his neighbors came to see him. Their faces were very sober, and they told father that he must not build his home down in the bottom land but that he must build it above the snake line. Then they described to him what would happen in the spring when the freshets came washing down brush and driftwood carrying hundreds of snakes. It would be entirely too dangerous to live near the river. They said, 'All of us must build our homes up on the hill above the snake line.'"

Russell Conwell had a unique talent for seeing great spiritual truths in the little everyday experiences of life. So, with all of the power of his great personality, he used this instance to point out to us the importance of building our individual lives high above the sordid. He went on to say, "There are probably very few people who are traveling the broad road which leads to destruction as the result of deliberately choosing that way of life. Most of those who live in the lowlands were as innocent as my father of the dangers surrounding them and found it out too late. I have never known a drunkard," he said, "who intended to be one. They were on that road that leads to destruction for one of two reasons. Either they were ignorant of the dangers of taking that first drink, or they had failed to make a definite dedication of their lives to the Master's way of living."

2 A second elective is stated in the question of Pilate, "What shall I do with Jesus?" Holman Hunt made this truth that we have a choice about Jesus live forever. When Jesus comes

24

gently knocking, we can open the door or we can leave it shut. There is no earthly power that can make us accept Jesus and his forgiveness, and here again God will not use his divine power, for this is the realm of electives. We have all sinned and we all stand in need of forgiveness. We can choose to pay the penalty of our wickedness or we can accept God's gracious plan of salvation and let the blood of Jesus Christ cleanse us from all sin.

John Maynard tells the story of his own conversion in a most interesting way. He said: "I was full of mischief, mixed with some meanness, when I was a boy at school. It was a lot of fun to put a frog in the teacher's desk or to bring a pigeon to school under my shirt and turn it loose in the classroom. I admit I was to blame for some of the teachers leaving in the middle of the school session, and I made it hard for the school board to keep a teacher in that little red schoolhouse. Then one day the miracle happened. A lovely Christian, with a smile and a sense of humor, came to take over this school. She immediately won my heart. My mother and father looked at each other with raised eyebrows when I suddenly began to shine my shoes, wash my face, and comb my hair.

"Commencement time came. My mother and father received an invitation to come to the exercises. They had never been to that school before. Until now they were ashamed to go. After the exercises were over, the teacher pointed to a shelf that went around the room and said to the parents: 'The children's work is arranged alphabetically. If you want to take a look at it, you may.'" John said: "I hung my head when I thought of that copybook. Before this teacher came, I had written on it upside down and crosswise and had put a few pictures here and there. Finally, I peeped up to see Mother and Father looking at that copybook, and my face went crimson. To my astonishment, there were no frowns on their faces. Father and Mother were smiling; he had his arm around her shoulders, and apparently they were delighted. When they moved away, I tipped over and looked at the copybook myself, and lo! someone had cut out all of the ugly pages, leaving only my best. Then I felt an arm around my shoulders, and I looked up to see this beautiful Christian teacher. With a smile she asked, 'John, do you know who taught me how to do that?' When I shook my head, she answered her own question, 'Jesus taught me.' Then she asked if I didn't want Jesus to wipe out all of the ugly things in my past life and forgive me for them. That is when I gave my life to Christ." How can anyone choose otherwise about this wonderful elective?

Third, an elective that we can choose is our destination. A few years ago one of the greatest baseball players of all time, and one of the finest men, was the outstanding hero of the World Series. His name is Pepper Martin. He received a truckload of fan mail from all over America. His hitting was phenomenal in every game. He was credited with being the most valuable and outstanding player of the Series. A group of reporters cornered him after the last game for an interview. They were generous in their compliments and expressions of admiration. Laughter and good will filled the hour. Then one of them asked him a serious question, "Pepper, now that you have won the World Series singlehanded, what do you want more than anything else in the world?" His answer startled them, for he said, after quietly thinking a few moments, "Above everything else in the world I want to go to heaven." They laughed uproariously; but Pepper Martin's face became very serious, and he stilled their laughter by quietly looking each one of them in the eye. Then, in the same calm voice he said: "What's so funny about that? I *do* want above everything else to go to heaven. I want to live so right that when I come to the end of life there won't be any question about where I am going to spend eternity." You can choose your destination. You alone will make this choice.

Dr. Kyle Yates, one of the great, lovable preachers of our denomination, made this truth very plain in a sermon he preached in our church some time ago. He startled many people when he said: "There is a difference between salvation and redemption. Redemption is God's part in the plan of salvation. When Jesus died on Calvary, he paid in full the penalty for our sins, and as he said on the cross, "It is finished." Our part in God's marvelous plan is the acceptance of this redemption. This is an elective. Unless we accept the redemption that God has put in his divine bank for us, we cannot spend eternity in heaven. "There is none other name under heaven given among men, whereby we must be saved."

A wealthy man had a son who was very wilful and a bit wild. He said one day, most emphatically, that he did not intend to go to college. His father pointed out all of the advantages of a college education and reasoned with him for quite a while. When the son still refused, his father said to him: "Son, I have put in the bank to your account $10,000. It is yours. There is only one stipulation. The checks must be made out to some university." So God has placed in his divine bank redemption for all. The conditions are simple and sublime and not hard to understand. He asks us only to believe, repent, and accept his Son as our Saviour. Heaven is within the reach of everyone. How can we refuse so great a salvation?

Guide us, dear Lord, in our choices. Help us not to take the wrong fork in the road. May thy will be the deciding factor in our plans always. Amen.

The elder unto the well-beloved Gaius, whom I love in the truth. Beloved, I wish above all things that thou mayest prosper and be in health, even as thy soul prospereth. For I rejoiced greatly, when the brethren came and testified of the truth that is in thee, even as thou walkest in the truth. I have no greater joy than to hear that my children walk in truth. Beloved, thou doest faithfully whatsoever thou doest to the brethren, and to strangers; Which have borne witness of thy charity before the church: whom if thou bring forward on their journey after a godly sort, thou shalt do well: because that for his name's sake they went forth, taking nothing of the Gentiles.

3 JOHN 1–7

4

Spiritual Prosperity

This third letter that John wrote is not a general epistle. It is a personal letter written to one of the Christian saints of John's time. Four times John called him "beloved," and the splendid things he said to him would warm the heart of any man. His name was Gaius, and he was evidently a pillar in the church. One sentence in the letter gives much food for thought. It is a wish or a prayer and reads like this: "Beloved, I wish above all things that thou mayest prosper and be in health, even as thy soul prospereth."

Gaius' life had reached such a high level of spirituality that John's wish "above all things" was that his prosperity and good health might be pulled up to balance with his spiritual life. I wonder how many of us could get down on our knees and ask God to bless us in health and give us prosperity even as we prosper spiritually? Would it be a dangerous prayer? John was thinking how wonderful it would be for Gaius if his life were balanced.

In other words, John's wish for Gaius was that he have a full-rounded, beautifully balanced life. John's great clarity of vision enabled him to see that the happiest and finest life will be the perfectly balanced life. Gaius may have been in bad health and his usefulness in the kingdom work jeopardized. Or reverses in his economic life may have threatened to handicap him. John was putting his finger on one of the most important laws of the universe, the law of balance. Every scientist, every physicist, and every skilled mechanic knows how important this balance is in the mechanical world.

I had this brought home to me very clearly by an automobile mechanic. I drove my car into his big shop because I was having difficulty steering it. I told him that when I got up to fifty or sixty miles an hour the steering wheel vibrated terribly. With his hands behind him he walked around in front of the car and looked intently at both front wheels; then he said, "How long have you had those new tires?" I told him, "Just a day." His next question was, "Did they balance the wheels when they mounted those tires?" When I told him, "No, I purchased them in a little town over on the desert," he smilingly said: "I think I know what is your trouble. The wheels are not balanced." A half hour later, after he had placed several little weights on each wheel, he suggested that we run it out on the road and see how it steered now. All of the vibration was gone. The car ran smoothly and steered easily. As we rode back to his shop, I asked him why it was so important to have the wheels balanced. He looked at me in astonishment, "Don't you know about the law of balance?" Pointing at the power plant, he said, "If one of those big flywheels in the electric plant over there was not in perfect balance, it would either shake that shop down or it would climb out of its moorings and run away."

This same law of balance is written all over God's world. When God created the earth, he gave it a perfect balance, so that it could turn its 25,000 miles in twenty-four hours without a tremor or a vibration. When he created us in his image, the law of balance was strictly observed. In the blood stream there is a ratio of white and red corpuscles. That balance must be kept. One of the first things the doctor looks at when we are ill is a drop of blood. Sometimes it is necessary for us to take large doses of medicine to kill the dangerous bacteria, and then the doctor tells us we must follow with another prescription that will help restore the balance of good bacteria that we need.

Even in the field of nature the law of balance is all important. In the popular book *Man Does Not Stand Alone* Cressy Morrison makes this very clear:

How strange is the system of checks and balances which has prevented any animal, no matter how ferocious, how large, or subtle, from dominating the earth since the age of trilobites and probably not then. Man only has upset this balance of nature by moving plants and animals from place to place, and he has immediately paid a severe penalty in the development of animal, insect, and plant pests. . . . Many years ago a species of cactus was planted in Australia as a protective fence. The cactus had no insect enemies in Australia and soon began a prodigious growth. The march of the cactus persisted until it had covered an area approximately as great as England, crowded the inhabitants out of the towns and villages, and destroyed their farms, making cultivation impossible. No device which the people discovered could stop its spread. Australia was in danger of being overwhelmed by a silent, uncontrollable, advancing army of vegetation. The entomologists scoured the world and finally found an insect which lived exclusively on cactus, would eat nothing else, would breed freely, and which had no enemies in Australia. Here the animal conquered the vegetation and today the cactus pest has retreated, and with it all but a small protective residue of the insects, enough to hold the cactus in check forever.*

---

* A. Cressy Morrison, *Man Does Not Stand Alone* (New York: Fleming H. Revell Company, 1944), pp. 78–79. Used by permission.

So John's wish for Gaius is that his health and prosperity may be lifted to the level of his spiritual life that he might enjoy life to the fullest. Let any one of these falter and a man will not be at his best.

The second thought suggested by the text is a question. Would you dare pray for America this prayer that John prayed? Would you get down on your knees and ask God to bless America with health and prosperity just to the level of her spiritual prosperity and no higher? If God answered a prayer like that, we would have a depression that the world would talk about a hundred years from now. We would be bankrupt and miserable. Could you even pray for your own town or city that God would give them health and prosperity even as their souls prosper, or as they prosper spiritually?

Dr. M. E. Dodd came back from India some years ago and preached in the church which I was serving. He had the instant attention of all of us when he said: "I saw a juggernaut. All of my life I had heard the expression that if this or that happened to you, you would be crushed as flat as if a juggernaut had rolled over you. Then one day on a tour of a city in Southern Asia I saw a real Juggernaut. It was about eighty feet long, forty feet wide, and high up in the air it held a throne for a huge idol that weighed tons. The idol's name was Vishnu. There were no wheels on the Juggernaut; instead, there were about twenty-five huge rollers made out of great logs. The bark had been pealed off, and they had been polished. An axle ran through the center of the logs. I walked around it and said, 'Can it be moved?' I was told that it took a thousand men with long ropes to roll it. Innocent still, I asked, 'And where do they pull it and why?' And then my blood froze when they told me: 'They pull it down the main street of a village, and human sacrifices are made to the idol. Mothers throw their babies in front of the rollers. They open the prisons, and after binding the prisoners, they are thrown in front of the rollers. They bring the aged and the infirm who are no longer useful and offer them to the idol in the same way.' "

Dr. Dodd said: "Anger and resentment boiled up within me, and I said, 'If they rolled that thing down Texas Avenue in Shreveport and one single person was thrown under it, the people of the United States of America would tear Shreveport apart.' Then I lost all of my arrogance as I realized that there *is* a juggernaut in America—the liquor traffic that rolls down almost *every* street and crushes the happiness and the very life out of many a home. Innocent children have their hopes crushed flat under this fearful juggernaut."

I ask the question again: Would you pray that your home prosper and be in good health even as it prospers spiritually? Would it be dangerous? Is your home a little bit of heaven sent down from above? If Jesus was coming to be your guest, as he was in the home of Mary and Martha and Lazarus, would you hide some things in the closet or carry them quickly out back? Would you have to be careful to control your temper and your tongue? Or would you be delighted and at ease because your home prospers spiritually?

The superintendent of one of our Baptist hospitals, speaking at Massanetta Springs, Virginia, on the importance of keeping our homes Christian, related this heartbreaking incident. "A little boy was brought into our emergency ward last week, mangled by a truck. He lived only a few hours, and it was my sad duty to go out to his home and tell his parents what had happened. When I arrived, his little sister was sitting on the front steps crying. When I asked her what was the matter, she told me that her brother had been hit by a

33

truck and they had taken him away. I told her I wanted to see her mother and father. She just pointed to the front door, which stood open. There was no answer to my knock, so I just walked in and knocked on the next door. Then I called and still received no answer. I pushed the door open. The house was a mess. Both mother and father were dead drunk. No amount of calling roused either of them. I went back and sat down by the little girl. My heart went out to her. What chance did she have for any happiness?" You couldn't have prayed John's prayer for Gaius in that home. The sad part of it is that there are homes so like this one all across this beloved country of ours.

The last question that comes out of John's prayer—and maybe it is the most important of all—is, would you pray this prayer for yourself? If we cannot pray this prayer for ourselves, we most likely will find that the balance has been upset by some dominant passion. I am not using the word "passion" in a sordid sense, but I am thinking of it in the sense of anything, however fine and good, that we allow to absorb our interest, our time, and our energy. That dominant passion may be something as wonderful as music. It may be something as needful as study. It may be something as worthy as the medical profession. It may be something as important as the work of scientists. But whatever thing we allow to demand all of us to the exclusion of our spiritual welfare, that thing is the dominant passion that can spoil the happiness of our whole lives and keep us from being able to pray this prayer. So let us examine ourselves carefully and do whatever is necessary to put back into its proper place a warm and friendly relationship with God.

Jesus once likened our lives to a house, and he emphasized the need of building it on a solid rock foundation. Otherwise,

34

when the floods came and the winds blew and the rain descended and beat upon that house, it might fall.

The sociologists tell us there are four cornerstones that should be made of solid rock if this house of ours does not sag. John pinpointed three of them in this one verse, namely, health, prosperity, and spirituality. The other one, relationships, was mentioned oftentimes by both John and Jesus. "Love thy neighbour as thyself." "Do unto others as you would that they should do unto you." "Forgive us our debts as we forgive our debtors." There is a danger in leaving out any one of these four important factors if we are going to enjoy the abundant life that Jesus talked about. Omit any of these, and we may miss one of the choice blessings that God promises us in the gospel.

In the early days of my ministry, while I was a country preacher in North Carolina, I met one of God's own saints, Josiah Elliott. He, too, was a country preacher for over fifty years, and he raised the level of spiritual living over a great section of the state he loved. In the last two or three years of his life, when he couldn't preach or even leave his home, he lived on the fat of the land. Although he had never saved a cent of money, he had invested in sending young ministerial students through college. He even mortgaged his home five times, and the five boys for whom it was done paid back every cent of the money. They were the pallbearers at his funeral.

The people of the community built that proverbial road to his front door, and they kept his smokehouse and his pantry filled with all the good things to eat. It was not unusual to hear a pastor say on a Sunday morning in one of those country churches which Josiah Elliott had served, "Let's take a love offering today for Brother Josiah." Propped up in bed, the grand old man with his long gray-white beard looked like a prophet. People came, not only to bring him something nice, but they came to kneel by his bed and ask him to pray for them. I can still feel his hand on my head as I knelt with my face in the crazy quilt and heard him earnestly ask God to make me a good preacher and keep me humble. Josiah Elliott prospered in health; he prospered materially, for he wanted for nothing; he prospered spiritually; and the crowds that came smiling with gifts assured him of their affection and love. They did unto him *even as* he had done unto them. They brought him happiness and peace of mind. He could pray this prayer of John's.

Father, may we so live that this great prayer may be prayed for us. Amen.

And she brought forth her firstborn son, and wrapped him in swaddling clothes, and laid him in a manger; because there was no room for them in the inn. And there were in the same country shepherds abiding in the field, keeping watch over their flock by night. And, lo, the angel of the Lord came upon them, and the glory of the Lord shone round about them: and they were sore afraid. And the angel said unto them, Fear not: for, behold, I bring you good tidings of great joy, which shall be to all people. For unto you is born this day in the city of David a Saviour, which is Christ the Lord.

LUKE 2:7–11

5

The Divinely Directed Drama

The story of the birth of Jesus is a drama. It is a divinely directed drama. It might rightly be called God's great drama. Someone has referred to it as being conventional in that there are three parts. I think it would be nearer correct to state that it is of the pattern which the conventional dramas have followed. It is well known that the first plays were shown in the churches. Our Christian fathers used plays to portray scenes that came from the word pictures of Jesus or from the great lessons presented by the Old Testament. There is one thing that should never be forgotten: this drama of the birth of Jesus is filled with the supernatural. The miraculous cannot be left out of any one of the three parts. They fall to pieces immediately if we omit the miracle that is in every one of them.

The first part is not beautiful. The scene is laid in Bethlehem, and the cold, hard sentence "There was no room for them in the inn" fills us with resentment.

Some twenty years ago I read a sermon on the little inn in Bethlehem. It made a lasting impression on me. The minister drew a most vivid picture of the busy innkeeper in the lobby of the small hotel in Bethlehem. He described the jostling crowd and the new travelers as they arrived. The innkeeper and all of the guests had one thing in common—they wanted the thing Jesus later called "abundant life." Each followed his profession or occupation, trying earnestly to get a little more out of life. Every guest demanded of the innkeeper the very best he could get. Then the preacher had a four-line refrain following each demand.

First, there came a Roman officer with his retinue of servants. Arrogantly, he demanded the best. His goal was always to squeeze a little more life out of each day, and while he searched blindly for some little extra thrill,

> "In a stable across the way,
> In a manger filled with hay,
> Wrapped in swaddling clothes there lay
> *The Lord of life.*"

Then a group arrived, among whom was a high political official, a wealthy sheik, and a courtesan. One glance at them and you knew their profession had one single aim—to get the most out of life. They also wanted the best rooms in the house. They wanted an abundance of the sweets of life, and every day they hunted for something that would add more zest and more satisfaction to life, while

> "In a stable across the way,
> In a manger filled with hay,
> Wrapped in swaddling clothes there lay
> *The Lord of life.*"

This little sentence, "There was no room," has stirred the indignation of Christian people from the time it was written down to this very day. Our resentment has included everybody in Bethlehem, and especially has it centered on the innkeeper and the people who slept in the comfortable beds. It has been the subject of many sermons, and it always has raised the question, and it is a good question, in the minds of all of us, "Have *I* made room in my life and in my home for Jesus?" Do I consider him and his wishes in all the things I do? Do I consult him about my plans? Is my dedication so complete that I will go where he leads me and do the things he bids me do?

Dr. John L. Hill, speaking at Massanetta Springs, Virginia, told this most interesting incident. In substance he said: "While I was a student in a university in the city of New York, there was a laymen's evangelistic effort. Services were held in the big Metropolitan Opera House every night for two weeks. The opera house was packed night after night. More than six hundred people comprised the choir and sat on the platform, with the seats built almost up to the ceiling. On the last night one of the fine Christian bankers was presiding. After the last message had been brought, he walked out to the front of the platform and said, 'Our program is over, but I do not dare close this meeting without presenting to you a very famous man who is sitting here with us.' Then he turned and said, 'Gypsy Smith, come over here and say whatever you want to say to this crowd.' "

Dr. Hill said, "I immediately sat forward on the edge of my seat. I had never seen Gypsy Smith, and I was tense with excitement. A quiet, broad-shouldered, black-haired man rose and smilingly walked to the front of the platform. Without a word, he stretched out his hands as if in supplication, and lifting his face toward heaven, he began to sing in a deep, rich voice, 'Where He leads me I will follow, I'll go with Him, with Him all the way." He sang the chorus through, and then with his hands he motioned for us to join him and sing

41

the chorus again. We just lifted the roof off of that opera house with that grand old hymn, 'Where He leads me I will follow, I'll go with Him, with Him all the way.' Then he lifted his hand for silence and, speaking with a voice that was full of emotion, said, 'When we can give to Christ the privilege of leading our lives every day, when we can bring him into our plans, life will be beautiful.' "

It was sad that the little inn at Bethlehem had no room for Jesus; yet it is sadder still that all around us there are people who leave God out of their lives entirely.

In the second part of this drama we have the heart of the whole Christmas story. It is stated in two short sentences. It is so fitting that these sentences should be spoken by an angel, one of God's own messengers, instead of by human lips. "Behold, I bring you good tidings of great joy, which shall be to all people. For unto you is born this day in the city of David a Saviour, which is Christ the Lord." This is *the* Christmas story. All the balance of the record is just background. Without this tremendous, indescribable fact everything else is meaningless. It is hard to understand why at Christmas time we pay so much attention to the trimmings and the tinsel, which form only the fringe of the great reality. We joyously sing carols, as the angels did; we give gifts, as the Wise Men did; but we neglect to emphasize the great truth that the center of Christmas is this unspeakable Gift—a Saviour is born.

To many of us the word "Saviour" carries with it the promise that we can be saved from the penalty of our sins. And the words of Paul come back to us, "There is none other name under heaven given among men, whereby we may be saved." He is talking about the salvation of our souls; he is talking about eternity. He is telling us that when we stand before the

42

judgment seat of God, Jesus will be our intercessor; that he will stand in our stead, and as Isaiah said, "He was wounded for our transgressions, he was bruised for our iniquities: . . . with his stripes we are healed. . . . The Lord hath laid on him the iniquity of us all." It makes us humble and deeply grateful. The message of the angels is true, and a glorious message it is.

This big truth was beautifully illustrated recently by one of our missionaries to the Gaza Strip, Mrs. Jane McRae. She told us of receiving a shipment of bundles of clothes that were sent from America to her school children. Each bundle was carefully wrapped and marked as to whether it was for a boy or for a girl. She had to unwrap each package and take out the little Testament that had been enclosed, because there was a severe penalty attached to distributing religious litera-ture unless it was requested. She placed all of the Testaments in a gunny sack to carry them from the school to her home. As she went along the street, a gang of boys snatched the sack from her hands and, after running a little way, dumped it into the street to see what they had. Disgusted because it wasn't food, they scattered the Testaments in the road. This resulted in her being arrested for distributing Christian literature, and she was ordered to appear in court the next day.

At two o'clock the next morning there was a knock at her door. When she opened it, she found a woman and a beauti-ful young girl, who was a student in her school. The girl told her that her father, who was a captain in the Arab army, wanted to talk to her at once. There was such urgency and fear in the young lady's voice that Mrs. McRae dressed and went over to the captain's home. He asked her to tell him the whole story. When she had finished, he said: "Because you are a

43

woman, it will be a disgrace for you to appear in court. You will lose your usefulness and the respect of everyone in the city. They will never forget it." He walked the floor for awhile and then said, "I will stand in your stead." She didn't realize what it would cost him to stand in her stead before the tribune, and it was days later when she learned that it meant disgrace for him too, and demotion. She never saw him or his lovely daughter again. She found that by saying a word in her behalf he had been banished from his country. Then with her voice choking with emotion, Mrs. McRae repeated, "He stood in my stead." That is what a Saviour means. He came to save us, not from disgrace or shame, but from our sins and punishment. He came to stand in our stead at God's judgment day.

The third part of the drama is truly the climax. The Wise Men, richly and gorgeously dressed, came from afar and laid at the feet of Jesus their priceless gifts. Then they knelt and worshiped. This scene has no resentment in it, nor is there any fear, like that of the shepherds. There are many lessons in this picture, but to me the two most striking are the following.

They brought the best that they had and laid it at the feet of Jesus. I think that Charles Kingsley must have been reading this account of the Wise Men when he wrote the adorable story of *The Littlest Angel*. You remember how it went. The littlest angel was out of place in heaven. His halo was always awry. He was forever late and entirely too noisy. He was always blundering. When God wanted to give a gift to his Son on earth, he asked everybody in heaven to bring their choicest offering and let him make a selection. The littlest angel tried to write a poem, but he failed. Then he tried to write a song, but he couldn't do that either. So he finally decided, with

44

some tears and distress, that he would bring the only thing he had, the little box of keepsakes he had brought from earth. When he placed it down beside the majestic presents the others had brought, it looked very small and ridiculous; but when God reached his hand for it, it suddenly glowed like burnished gold and quickly was transformed into a sparkling, scintillating gem.

This example of the Wise Men in bringing their precious gifts and laying them at the feet of Jesus has inspired us through the centuries to give God the best that we have. God needs our individual personalities; he needs our talents; he needs our possessions. And when we lay them at his feet, they, too, are transformed, even as the littlest angel's gift, into something that will make the world finer and better. The psalmist has a sentence which should give us much thought, "He . . . bringeth forth his fruit in his season." As Paul said, we cannot all be teachers nor can we all work miracles, but we can all bear our own fruit in our own season.

The second lesson is the unconscious influence that these Wise Men have exerted across the centuries. It never occurred to them that for two thousand years and more the thing they did would be told in story and song. They had no thought of playing any part in the world's greatest drama. They were not trying to do anything spectacular. They had no idea that they were preaching an unforgettable sermon. They did not know that the greatest artists of the world would spend months painting their portraits and that millions of people would stand for hours in adoration. We Christian people often are not conscious of playing any part in the life of someone else and yet, unknown to us, we may be playing the star role in somebody's life. What is more, we may never find it out. On the other hand, it may come back to us, as the bread

45

that is cast on the waters, to refresh us in some hour of our need.

Let me illustrate. Into a church in the city of New York one Sunday morning there walked a young man who was a bit disheveled, and his hair was uncombed. He had walked the streets all night. He didn't much care what people thought of his looks, for he was deeply disturbed. He had lost his grip on the meaning and the purpose of life. He had lost his contact with God; doubt and fear had come into his mind. He was so miserable that he had begun to wonder whether life was worthwhile or not. Finally, he decided he would go in and sit down on the back seat of this church and listen one more time to a sermon. When the pastor said, "Let us bow our heads in prayer," he didn't move or bow his head at all. He didn't shut his eyes but looked around at the others, and then for the first time he saw his science professor across the aisle.

The professor had leaned forward, head bent in the attitude of humble worship. The student watched him, and when the prayer was over, he saw that the professor's face was quiet and restful. Peace and contentment were written all over it. The student afterward said that he never heard a word of the sermon that was preached from the pulpit because of the deep impression his professor had made upon him. The professor was entirely unconscious of the fact that the student was even there and did not know until years later what had happened. The student, slipping out quietly after the service, said to himself, "If that great wizard in science believes in God and knows there is a God, and believes in prayer and has peace written all over him, then it must be true."

Years later coming back on furlough, a medical missionary now, he went up to the old professor's home and told him the story. For the first time the professor knew that he had played the star part in this great missionary's life. The Wise Men never knew, and maybe you and I will never know when we are playing the star part in somebody's life drama. We need to walk as ever in the great taskmaster's eye.

Dear Lord, may we live so close to thee that our actions and our words may make life sweeter for all who walk beside us. Amen.

O give thanks unto the Lord; for he is good: for his mercy endureth for ever. O give thanks unto the God of gods: for his mercy endureth for ever. O give thanks to the Lord of lords: for his mercy endureth for ever. To him who alone doeth great wonders: for his mercy endureth for ever. To him that by wisdom made the heavens: for his mercy endureth for ever. To him that stretched out the earth above the waters: for his mercy endureth for ever. To him that made great lights: for his mercy endureth for ever: the sun to rule by day: for his mercy endureth for ever: the moon and stars to rule by night: for his mercy endureth for ever.

PSALM 136:1–9

6

The Big Things of Life

Psalm 136 is unique. No other psalm follows its pattern. It is comprised of twenty-six verses, and there is one clause repeated in every one of those twenty-six verses. In the King James Version that clause reads, "For his mercy endureth for ever." One of the revised versions translates it, "For his steadfast love endures for ever." *The Interpreter's Bible,* commenting on it, has this sentence, ". . . *hésedh,* though translated 'kindness,' implies 'fidelity' or 'loyalty' and has more facets than can be rendered by a single English word." Still another commentary translates it "bountiful love." Evidently, there is no English equivalent for the Hebrew word, and it may take all of these translations together to enable us to see its full meaning. But there is no mistaking the purpose of this passage. It was written to express a gratitude that was so big the writer's heart was bursting with it. The psalm opens with, "O give thanks unto the Lord; for he is good. . . . O give thanks unto the God of Gods. . . . O give thanks unto the Lord of lords," and it ends with the same strain, "O give thanks unto the God of heaven: for his mercy endureth for ever." In between these exclamations the psalmist enumerates a number of things for which he is grateful.

49

To me, there is one supreme message in the psalm. It is not spelled out in any verse. I saw it only after I had read the psalm quietly and worshipfully, then closed my Bible to meditate awhile on that which I had read. It seems to me that the essence of the psalm and its deepest message is that the writer was trying to express his gratitude to God for the *big things of life*. He was thanking God for creating the heavens and stretching out the earth above the waters, and for making the great lights—the sun, the moon, the stars. He was thanking God for deliverance from Egypt, for supplying all the needs of his Chosen People. His mind had soared far above the trivial. There is no reference to the little vexations and irritations that come to us in the course of the day, and in his mind he was high above the earth. As you read it you are reminded of the words of Jesus, "And I, if I be lifted up from the earth, will draw all men unto me." One of the most wonderful things about Christianity is that it lifts us up and helps us to get a proper perspective of the intricate little byways of life. Many times we need to pray a prayer to God to help us not to let the molehills hide the mountains or the trees keep us from seeing the forest. We miss seeing the snow-capped mountains that reach toward heaven because we let our eyes get too close to the little bumps in the road of life.

Mr. R. L. Middleton, in one of his recent delightful books, has a story about Clarence Powell. It goes about like this. "Clarence Powell gave one of the best testimonies in prayer meeting that I ever heard. He is a well-to-do man now, but there were days when the going was rough. He was then a construction worker and made good money when he worked, but for quite a while there had been no work and his finances were in bad shape. In his testimony he said: 'I had six children, and it was time for school to start in the fall. The shoes of three of them were entirely worn out. The boys had been using their feet for brakes on their wagons as they coasted down the hill; the little girl had been skipping rope, and their shoes were in ruins. While I was fretting about this and wondering where I could get some credit, my wife told me that the washing machine had hopelessly broken down. In desperation I searched the papers to see if there was a second-hand washing machine for sale. I finally found one and immediately went to look at it.

" 'When I got to the right address, I hesitated to go in. The house was so large and imposing a little resentment boiled up in my heart. When I did walk into the kitchen, I just stopped and stood astonished. Everything was so beautiful. There was a dishwashing machine, a combination washer and dryer, a Deepfreeze, a refrigerator, and an electric stove. I stood there thinking how happy my wife would be if she had a kitchen like this and wondering why some people had all the good luck anyhow. The man and his wife offered to sell me the washing machine for just a few dollars, and my expressions of gratitude just bubbled out. I even told them about the children's shoes—how they had worn them out dragging them on the road and skipping rope, and what a tough time I was having to make ends meet. And then I said to them: "It must be nice to have everything so convenient. You must be very happy."

" 'Then I became aware that the wife had turned a little pale, and after looking at her husband with a pained expression, she had started out of the room. A little sob escaped her as she went through the door. I asked her husband if I had said something wrong. For a few moments he didn't answer. He was looking at the floor. Then he cleared his throat and said: "No, you didn't say anything wrong. You

51

were talking about the children's shoes being worn out. We have only one child, a little girl. She's never walked a step in her life. A pair of worn-out shoes would make *us* very happy."'

"Clarence Powell said, 'I went back home and went up to my room and closed the door. I got down on my knees and asked the Lord to forgive me for fretting about the little things. I got those three pairs of shoes and looked at them and smiled. I was so thankful for three pairs of worn-out shoes and for two boys that could ride a wagon and a girl that could skip a rope.'"

I repeat, the greatest message of this psalm to me is that it makes me conscious of the debt of gratitude I owe God for the big things of life. It makes me ashamed of the way I magnify the little irritations and frustrations.

One of the big things for which the psalmist was struggling to express his gratitude was that the steadfast love of God had given to his people such a rich heritage. For many years before the psalmist wrote these words his country had enjoyed freedom and liberty. No iron heel was grinding them down; no Egyptian slave whip was lashing their backs; no longer were they making bricks without straw. God's steadfast love had manifested itself in so many wonderful ways.

I listened recently to Brooks Hays, president of the Southern Baptist Convention, as he told us about his visit to Moscow and the one Baptist church in that big city. The Baptist people were not allowed to build another, nor were they allowed to have services any day except Sunday. He told us of the crowds that were packed outside the church as he approached it and how the center aisle had been kept open until he arrived. As he went in, the opening closed behind him as the group pushed and struggled to fill up the middle aisle and stand for an hour to worship God. Then the congregation was dismissed and almost had to be driven out of the church so that others might come in for the next service, which followed immediately. They had no Sunday school equipment and no place to teach their children except in the homes. There the religious instruction was left to the grandparents, for the mothers were forced to work.

He made us all feel a little guilty because we are not thankful enough for our rich heritage and the right to worship God unmolested. As we listened I think some of us saw our beautiful auditorium with new appreciation, and the music seemed a little more heavenly. Has God been too good to us, and has he given us too rich a heritage? Are we so spoiled that we care little for this priceless privilege? There are millions of people across the world that would give almost anything for the blessings that we so easily forget. Did you thank God this morning for America? Did you thank him for your church? Did you thank him for the joy of sleeping unafraid last night and for the joy of getting up this morning and having a home and a place to work and a task to do? I wonder sometimes if God doesn't let disasters come to us in order that we may value the things that we take for granted.

Dr. McCracken, minister of the Riverside Church in New York City, speaking to a Rotary Club at the time of Austria's terrible trouble, made this thoughtful statement: "Austria is on her knees today. She is praying earnestly to God to help her in this hour of agony. She is praying him to send some other nation to rescue her people from being murdered. America isn't on her knees today. America is laughing and singing to rock and roll music and looking eagerly to find some new way to be amused. Sunday is just a day for frolic. There are millions of people who are not even thinking of going to church and who seldom get down on their knees to thank God for anything, least of all for our country." Dr. McCracken ceased speaking for a moment and then in solemn, sad tones continued, spacing his words, "If suddenly over the top of us a few atomic bombs exploded, the rock and roll would be forgotten, and the frivolous, careless crowd would be frantically praying to God."

So many people pray only when they are afraid or in trouble, but in this psalm the writer was thanking God in an hour of prosperity. He's thanking God for the big things of life—the things we forget.

Another of the big things, not spelled out in this psalm but which comes drifting up like the fragrance of sweet perfume, is the feeling of joy and happiness. Immediately into your mind comes another sentence, which is in a psalm close by: "Make a joyful noise unto the Lord." Psalm 136 *is* a joyous noise. It was set to music and enjoys the distinction of being called the "great hallel." It was used at the Feast of the Passover and at the New Year's festival. One choir sang the first line of the verse and another choir answered, "His mercy endureth for ever." Nowhere in the psalm does the author say in words, "We thank thee, Lord, for the joy of our religion," but the whole message of the psalm is like a sweet savor that permeates the atmosphere. Joy is written all over it. It is just a step in thought from the joyous message of this psalm to the scene on the rolling hills of Bethlehem where the angel said to the shepherds, "Behold, I bring you good tidings of great joy, which shall be to all people." Among all the lovely things in Christianity for which we can be deeply thankful joy takes its place near the top. Christianity changes lives from miserable existence to joyous living.

When I left home for college to study for the ministry, my

aunt gave me a book of sermons written by Dr. G. H. Morrison. I am sure she knew I was going to have a hard time preparing a sermon and that I would need some help from one of the great old preachers. There is one sermon in the book that I still remember and cherish. In it Dr. Morrison sets in splendid contrast the right and the wrong attitude toward living a Christian life. He drew a picture of a man to whom his Christianity was a delight. Sunday was the great day of the week for him, and all through the week whenever the conversation touched on things religious, his countenance beamed. To him Christianity meant happiness and joy. Over against this the author set a man who went to church religiously but did so because of a sense of duty. Sunday was the worst day of the week for him. He never sang the hymns. His lips were tight pressed as he endured the services. He was like the man about whom one of my fellow pastors told me recently. After the Sunday night service this member of his church, walking home, heard the music of a Salvation Army meeting on a street corner. He stopped on the outskirts of the crowd to hear the trombone, the trumpet, and the singing. A sweet-faced little Salvation Army lassie smilingly asked him, "Are you a Christian?" His gruff answer was, "I hope so." Sensing that he didn't want to talk to her, she went around the crowd to where the leader stood, and because of the music she raised her voice to tell him about the stranger. Just then the music stopped, and her voice came clearly to him through the silence, "He said he hopes he is a Christian, but look at his face."

Someone has well said, "Our faces are oftentimes maps of our characters." Certainly, our countenances do often reflect the thoughts and the attitudes of our hearts. When Paul said, "Adorn the gospel," I am sure he meant that our actions and our attitudes should be so good that they automatically would be a silent witness for our Master and his love.

Recently I spoke at a loyalty banquet in one of the big cities of Louisiana. The dinner was arranged as a part of the financial program of the church, and the emphasis was on tithing. To me the most thrilling part of that program was the testimony given by a Christian layman. When he was introduced, the applause was thunderous. He was good to look at. He had iron-gray hair. Gentleness, kindness, and happiness were written all over his face. As the applause kept on, he just stood quietly and smiled and by-and-by lifted his hand in recognition of the tribute. This is about what he said: "When I was a boy of fourteen, I came home one Saturday with my first pay envelope. I didn't open it till I got home. Mother and I sat down at the kitchen table, and I poured the money out. There were thirteen one dollar bills and twenty cents. I thought it was the biggest pile of money I had ever seen. My mother said, 'What are you going to do with it, Son?' I told her, 'I am going to buy a pair of skates with some of it, and I am going to buy a pair of gloves. Then I want to buy you something, Mother.' 'What will you do with the balance of it?' she asked. I told her I thought I would start a savings account. Then, quietly smiling, she said, 'Aren't you going to give God a tithe of it?' 'Do I have to?' was my quick response. After a moment of silence she said: 'No, Son, it is your money, and you don't have to give God any of it, but your father and I tithe. We get a lot of pleasure out of it, and I am sure that our tithing has had much to do with the kind of a home that you have. Suppose you go up to your room and think about it, and I would suggest you pray about it, then make your own decision.'

"I stayed upstairs a couple of hours. When I came down,

I went straight to Mother and asked her if she would answer a question for me. She said, 'Certainly, what is it?' 'Suppose I don't tithe. Suppose I don't give God any of it. What would happen to me?' She looked at me and soberly said, 'Nothing, Son, nothing now.' I was greatly relieved and stood there a moment before resuming the conversation. 'Mamma, what will happen if I do tithe?' Her face was beaming as she answered: 'That's what I wanted you to ask me. The same thing that's happened to your daddy and me. You will find more peace of mind, more joy, more satisfaction in being a good steward than in any one thing you will ever do. The whole world will be sweeter to you; you will love to say your prayers; you will be proud of your religion; and you will know that God is proud of you. You will grow strong spiritually. Your Christianity and your church will be very precious to you.' "

The speaker stood there a bit choked up, and the eight hundred people in front of him had their emotions deeply stirred. When he could talk again, he said in a husky voice: "You know, it makes me tremble, tremble, tremble, like that old song says, when I think, 'Suppose I hadn't started to tithe?' Out of the bottom of my heart I can say that nothing in the world has meant as much to me as my relationship to my Heavenly Father, and I doubt if I would ever have enjoyed this relationship if I hadn't started tithing." The joy of his salvation and the joy of his heart were written all over his face. He belonged to God, and God belonged to him.

Dear Lord, the little things of life spoil our usefulness and hide the big blessings that thou hast given us. Give us eyes that can see and ears that can hear. Amen.

Whereunto I am appointed a preacher, and an apostle, and a teacher unto the Gentiles. For the which cause I also suffer these things: nevertheless I am not ashamed: for I know whom I have believed, and am persuaded that he is able to keep that which I have committed unto him against that day. Hold fast the form of sound words, which thou hast heard of me, in faith and love which is in Christ Jesus. That good thing which was committed unto thee keep by the Holy Ghost which dwelleth in us.

2 Timothy 1:11–14

Three Tremendous Truths

"Whereunto I am appointed . . . a teacher of the Gentiles. For the which cause I also suffer these things: . . . for I know whom I have believed, and am persuaded that he is able to keep that which I have committed unto him against that day." In these few lines Paul has pressed the answer to some of life's biggest questions. Paul was writing a letter to Timothy, but the letter doesn't belong to Timothy alone. It belongs to all of us. God is using Paul to give us three tremendous truths. Every one of them is clearly stated. There is not a superfluous word, nor is there a single letter omitted. This is indeed a marvelous passage of Scripture. Look at these three sentences.

I

"For the which cause I also suffered these things." In "these things" Paul is referring to the fact that he is in chains and a prisoner. In a wider sense they refer to all the sufferings, the shipwrecks, the beatings, and the stoning which he endured in the past. Very clearly Paul states: "Whereunto I am appointed a preacher, and an apostle, and a teacher of the Gentiles. For the which cause I also suffer these things."

Here, indeed, is a theological gem. If we could get this wonderful truth deep down in our hearts, it would save us from so much mental agony. So often when some calamity comes to us, some frustration or some disappointment, the first prayer we offer to God is a question: "Lord, what have I done to deserve this?" Our minds go racing back across the past. We find some sin that we committed or some great omission in our lives, and we wonder if this is the punishment. It doesn't even occur to us, as the tears roll down our cheeks or as we stand stunned, that maybe this is a part of God's plan and that by-and-by we will understand that this may be one of the "all things" that work together for good to them that love God. We don't for the moment see that the awful thing that has happened to us may be the direct or indirect result of some assignment God had given to us. It may even be the direct result of a God-given task well done.

This is not a "proof text." It is written all through the Bible. We need to go back and read a few sentences spoken by some of God's great servants. For instance, verse 9 of the first chapter of Revelation reads like this: "I John, . . . was in the isle that is called Patmos, for the word of God, and for the testimony of Jesus Christ." John isn't complaining; there is no resentment in his heart as he states simply: "I am a prisoner, exiled to a lonely, barren island because of my testimony of Jesus Christ and because I have been faithful and loyal and true to the Great Commission that Jesus gave me. I am his witness. I witnessed so well, so enthusiastically, that it was necessary for the enemies of Christianity to silence me." This is just what Paul is saying also, "For the which cause I also have suffered."

Or we might turn to the Old Testament and look at a pathetic and dramatic picture of Moses. He has gone away from the camp to a quiet place and is talking to God about these obstreperous people who continually provoked the patience of God and himself. God is angry with the children of Israel and is telling Moses that he is going to destroy them, and Moses is suffering mental anguish and agony. His sentence is, "If thy presence go not with me, then carry us not up hence." He even offers himself as a living sacrifice if God will just forgive again these wilful, disobedient, unruly people. Moses, just as Paul, is suffering these things because he is good and because he is trying to do what God wants him to do.

It will be well for us when we suffer for something in connection with the performance of the task assigned by our Heavenly Father to learn that we are in a glorious company. We need to get it forever in our hearts that all of the tribulations and trials, all of the frustrations in life, and all of the heartaches of life are not necessarily the consequences of some transgression of our own, but like Jesus, nailed to the cross, we are suffering with him for the sins of others. The high and stately pulpit from which Paul preached was built layer upon layer, board upon board, stone upon stone, by the afflictions that Paul suffered for the gospel of Jesus Christ. It is a majestic picture that comes to us as we read these lines, and with our mind's eye we see Paul standing tall and noble, saying: "Timotheus, Timotheus, all of these things I suffer because I was called to be an apostle and a preacher and a teacher. God let me suffer these things that others might be saved and that my voice might be penetrating enough to reach down a hundred centuries."

Beloved, this is a glorious truth, this is shouting ground. We should hug this to our hearts. It can be an inspiration and a comfort in the darkest hours that come to us.

Let me illustrate it with an incident that happened forty

61

years ago and yet is so vivid. I was a young country preacher in eastern North Carolina, and on a hot, sultry day I was driving my horse and buggy along a deep, sandy road when I met the Methodist preacher who had the same circuit. He said: "Roy, you look tired and jaded. If you are not in a hurry, turn around and follow me back about half a mile to that home that you just passed under the big, shady oak trees. A little old lady lives there who will have a pitcher of cool lemonade and some cookies. She has wanted to meet you anyhow." I followed him back. We unhitched our horses to let them rest, and we went into a high-ceilinged old home, cool and delightful. A little old lady on crutches cheerfully invited us in and told us to wait just a minute, that she had had some refreshments for us. When she came back with them, she placed them on the table, took her glass of lemonade, and stood by the mantelpiece. I offered her my chair and then was embarrassed because she, smiling still, said: "You see, I can't sit down. I have iron braces from my feet to my shoulders." When I stammered out some words of sympathy and concern, she answered with these unforgettable words: "Don't be so concerned about me. I have an idea God needed someone down here to wear iron braces and smile and be happy to show his power to help in the troubles of life."

To be sure, God lets us suffer sometimes that we might be shaped and molded into a vessel fit to carry the gospel to others. I am sure it hurts the heart of God to let us suffer. But it takes the "diamond dust" of suffering to fit us for his mission, and so God allows it. Paul was blinded by the light on the Damascus road, "and he was three days without sight, and neither did eat nor drink."

I like the way that Dr. Ellis Fuller, pastor of the First Baptist Church of Atlanta, later president of the Southern Baptist seminary, illustrated this thought. He said: "I made a call in one of the fine Christian homes, and the mother said to me: 'Dr. Fuller, you know grown men and women are so like children, and children are so like them in many respects. For instance, I have two boys, and the older boy hasn't been well for a good many years. The younger boy is so husky and strong, and he outgrew the older boy. He's taller and bigger and heavier, and because he's got a little inferiority complex about being younger than his brother, he picks on him. I have quite a hard time with him. The other day I walked in the house just as this younger boy slapped the older one, and he hit him hard. When he saw me, he froze. He knew how many times I had punished him for that. I froze, too, and just stood there and looked at him. By-and-by his head dropped, and I walked away.

" 'A little while afterward I heard him behind me. He was shifting nervously from one foot to the other. Finally he said, "Mamma, can I help you in some way? Is there something I can do for you?" I told him I didn't need anything. I knew what he wanted. We grown people are just like that. We think we can pay God off with some little extra service when we've done something that has displeased him. I went on with the housework. Half an hour later, while I was sewing, I heard him come in again. I felt so sorry for him, but I knew he had to learn his lesson, and I just waited. I didn't look around. He said: "Mamma, the woodbox is about empty. Can I go get you some wood and fill it up?" I had to wait a moment before answering, because there was a lump in my throat. I said, "No, Son, I don't think we'll need any more wood today." I heard him turn around and start out. He got as far as the door, stopped again, and I looked around. When I did,

63

he burst into tears and, sobbing, he came running and put his arms around my waist. He said: "Mamma, I'm so sorry. Please forgive me. I won't ever do it again." Dr. Fuller, that's what God wants to hear us say.' " Dr. Fuller said, "As I looked at the tear-brimmed eyes of this mother, I knew that God suffered all the time Paul was suffering and that whenever he has to let us suffer in order to teach us some great lesson or shape us to fill some assignment, he suffers, too."

II

"I know whom I have believed." Paul was putting the emphasis on the verb *know*. There isn't anything in Paul's writings that would give us the impression that he was quoting someone else, that he believed this thing because someone else told him it was so. Paul's was a firsthand religion. We read in the Gospels that Jesus spoke "as one having authority." Well, Paul spoke as one having authority, too. Of course, he didn't have the authority that Jesus had, but he had a faith so strong that he continually spoke with a deep finality.

There was no hearsay in the things that Paul stated. He never said, "You have heard that it hath been said." He spoke directly. His religion was a vivid reality to him. The presence of God to him was very personal. God lived and moved all around him. This, I say, is one of the vital needs of all of us. To so many of us Christianity has been handed down as a package, either from our parents, our teachers, or our church, and we treat it as something we can have if we want it, but it is not a vital and necessary part of life. The personal experiences of Paul had convinced him of the omniscience and the omnipotence of God. So without any reservations he could state, "I know whom I have believed," or, "I can do all things through him which strengtheneth me."

A man in Dr. R. G. Lee's church at Memphis gave me a good illustration of this kind of faith and belief when he told me the story of the whale that was washed up on the shore at Miami Beach. He said: "They put that whale on a couple of flatcars and, after treating it with chemicals, sent it across the country and charged a fee to see it. It was in Oklahoma when I saw it. As I stood watching it and listening to the "old salt" who was conducting its tour, two men came up. One of them asked, 'How big is its throat?' The "old salt" took his pipe out of his mouth and answered: 'The whale's throat is the smallest part of him. That's the only little thing about a whale. It's just about big enough for him to swallow a good-sized grapefruit.' One of the men turned to the other a bit arrogantly and said: 'I told you so. I told you that story of Jonah and the whale wasn't so. This proves it.' The old sailor waited for the other man to answer, and when he didn't, he took his pipe out of his mouth again. 'Friends, let me tell you something. You don't know your Bible very well. You get your Bible and see what it says. It says that God prepared a great fish to swallow Jonah. In the first place, God prepared the fish to swallow Jonah. In the second place, if God had said he sent a whale, God could have made that whale's throat big enough to swallow a boxcar.' The "old salt" with a disgusted grunt turned and walked away." God to him was personal like he was to Paul. His faith was so strong that he could say with conviction, "I *know* whom I have believed."

III

"I am persuaded that he is able to keep that which I have committed unto him against that day." This sentence is the *therefore* in Paul's theology. He is saying in substance: "I *know* God. He is always true and faithful and never fails.

Also, I know he is omnipotent. I know he can do all things. Therefore, there is no fear in my heart. I can trust him with my life, which I have committed unto him." I have often wondered if that passage in the third chapter of Daniel wasn't very precious to Paul. Nebuchadnezzar had threatened to throw Shadrach, Meshach, and Abednego into the burning, fiery furnace if they didn't bow down and worship the image he had built. The three of them stood before the king, who held life and death in his hands, and fearlessly answered him: "We are not careful to answer thee in this matter. If it be so, our God whom we serve is able to deliver us from the burning fiery furnace, and he will deliver us out of thine hand, O king. But if not, be it known unto thee, O king, that we will not serve thy gods, nor worship the golden image which thou hast set up."

This is exactly what Paul is saying: "I am a prisoner, but I have no fear. I am persuaded that my God is able to keep me, but if he doesn't see fit to set me free from this Roman prison, that, too, will be all right." Paul's commitment was complete. He was willing for God to do anything with his life that fitted into the divine plan. He was not worried about the future. He never complained about the past. There is deep assurance written all over this passage of Scripture—assurance that whatever happened to him would be for the best and that nothing could happen without God's consent. What a wonderful thing it would be for the kingdom of God if all of us who are called by the name of Christian would make such a commitment to our Heavenly Father. What a wonderful thing it would be to us individually if our faith were as deep-rooted as this.

I read a most striking illustration of this kind of commitment just recently. A foreign mission board of another denomination was meeting to examine some candidates for the mission field. When they came down to the last one, the secretary of the board said to the other members: "Before I bring this last young lady in, I want to read to you a telegram that came from one of the professors in the seminary from which she graduated. The wire has bothered me, for I don't understand it. It reads like this: 'Be sure to ask her if she believes that Jesus Christ died on the cross to save us from our sins.' Immediately one of the members bounced out of his chair. "Mr. Secretary, if she doesn't believe that, she will never go out from this board as a missionary." His statement was followed by a dozen "amens."

Into this hostile atmosphere the young lady was called. The secretary controlled his voice and said quietly, "The first question we want to ask you is, Do you believe that Jesus died to save us from our sins?" Her answer completely floored them all. With strong conviction she said: "Yes, I believe that Jesus died to save us from our sins. Also, I believe with all of my heart that he expects some of us to die to save the world from its sins. I have given him my life, and if he needs for me to die on the mission field that others may have redemption and salvation, I am perfectly willing for it to be that way." It is a commitment like this that Paul made, and it was with that deep conviction that he spoke these words to Timothy: "I know whom I have believed, and am persuaded that he is able to keep that which I have committed unto him against that day."

Our Father which art in heaven, help us to understand thy ways. Make us willing to suffer even as Jesus did that thy kingdom may come in the hearts and lives of others. Amen.

But when ye pray, use not vain repetitions, as the heathen do: for they think that they shall be heard for their much speaking. Be not ye therefore like unto them: for your Father knoweth what things ye have need of, before ye ask him. After this manner therefore pray ye: Our Father which art in heaven, Hallowed be thy name. Thy kingdom come. Thy will be done in earth, as it is in heaven. Give us this day our daily bread. And forgive us our debts, as we forgive our debtors. And lead us not into temptation, but deliver us from evil: For thine is the kingdom, and the power, and the glory, for ever. Amen.

MATTHEW 6:7–13

8

Daily Bread

Dr. William Osler, who established Johns Hopkins School of Medicine, has often stated that his favorite text is, "Give us this day our daily bread." A few years ago he came over from England to deliver the Yale lectures. His first address began like this: "Young gentlemen, the president of your great university has requested me to tell you the secret of my success, as he calls it, in medicine. I'm a bit embarrassed, but I saw a good illustration of this so-called secret as I came across the Atlantic Ocean on a big, palatial liner. The captain was kind enough to invite me up on the bridge. For an hour we talked about generalities. Then he said: 'Let me show you something. This is one of the most wonderful ships that was ever built. See this panel of buttons? If I pushed this one, you would hear the rumbling of great steel bulkheads down in the bottom of the ship. They would close off the entire lower deck. If I touched this one, it would seal off the next level so that if we should strike something, knock a hole in the bottom or the side of the ship, I could seal off any or all of the lower decks. Or I could turn to this panel, touch this button and seal off the whole bow. This one would seal off the whole stern. It's really thrilling to listen to those

69

great bulkheads as they tremble and roll into their places.' "

The great doctor turned to the group of students at Yale and said: "Gentlemen, the body that you have is much more complicated, delicately balanced, and more wonderfully built than that ship, and you ought to be able, by-and-by, as you grow older to touch a control button and shut off the yesterdays with all their worries and cares. You ought to be able to touch another control button and seal off the tomorrows with all of their apprehensions and fears."

He continued: "When I was graduating in medicine, like some of you will be doing soon, and came up to the final examination, I was worried about where I was going to practice and if I could ever possibly make a living practicing medicine. I was so afraid of the examinations that I was walking the floor at night. One night I stopped my pacing long enough to pick up and read a little from one of Carlyle's essays. I found these words: 'You should not worry about the dim, unknown and unknowable future, but you should view the duty that is closest at hand and accomplish as best you can the task that needs to be done *this day.*' "

He said: "That sank into my heart. I stopped walking the floor and took an inventory of my problems. Which duty was closest at hand? The examinations were the first things. I took them and passed. Then my decision about locating was in front of me, and I made it. Gentlemen, I have learned to do the duty and the task that needs to be done *this day.* I have learned to touch a control button and seal off the yesterdays with their mistakes and victories, then touch another control and seal off the tomorrows."

Most certainly, Dr. Osler had learned a lesson that we all need to have as our very own. The weight of the yesterdays plus the weight of the tomorrows will be too heavy for us to

70

carry and ever do a good day's work today. There is a sense
in which we must live life one day at a time. Any day we
live may bring us face to face with forks in the road. The
decisions we make may easily affect our whole future. Therefore, this sentence, "Give us this day our daily bread," in the
prayer of Jesus is so very important. We need the kind of
daily bread that God alone can give us. I am sure that Jesus
was not limiting the definition of the word "bread" to physical food. He once called himself the "Bread of life." It was,
I think, spiritual food that Jesus had in mind when he said,
"Give us this day our daily bread." Meditate thoughtfully on
these words long enough and they will open to you a number
of delightful avenues.

The first one goes all the way back to God's creation of
the world. The account in Genesis is very specific. God did
not make the world in a single day. He could have called it
forth in a moment. But the record reads after each step: "The
evening and the morning were the first day," "the evening
and the morning were the second day," and "the evening and
the morning were the third day." It would seem that God
set for himself a *daily* task. Then he created man in his own
image and made him on the same pattern he himself had
used in creating the world. He gave him *daily needs*. Why
didn't he make us so we could eat and drink enough to last
us a month? Why can't we breathe into our lungs enough
oxygen to last us for a whole day? Why can't we sleep enough
at one time to last for ten months? No one can answer these
questions arbitrarily and with authority. We do not know
why God made the divisions in time and called them night
and day. We do not know all the reasons that he had for
creating man with a multitude of hungers and wants that
must be met day after day. We do know that God, in his in-

71

finite wisdom, knew that it was best for us to have life broken into summer and winter, day and night. He also knew that it was best for us to have certain hungers that would recur daily. It was not in his plans to let man lie down and sleep for a month at a time.

Another avenue leads away back in the Old Testament when God sent manna *daily* to the wandering children of Israel. They tried to hoard some so they wouldn't have to get up early and gather it every day. It spoiled. Some things must be done daily.

The other avenue that is opened by this verse is, of course, the most important. Just as we have daily physical needs, we have daily spiritual needs. God has used the same pattern of creation for our spiritual lives as he used for our physical lives. How can we have this spiritual food? I can think of three answers to that question.

Sometimes God sends this spiritual food in a strange and unexpected way. I read just the other day of a surgeon who had tried all day long to finish his work and get home on Christmas Eve to be with his wife and children. It was nine o'clock at night before he could leave the last patient. His wife met him at the door. It made her uneasy to see how tired and worn out he was. Wearily he said to her: "I'd planned to help the children trim the Christmas tree, and I was going to take them downtown. Oh, I guess I'm such a failure. I never can do the things I plan. I wanted to be with them so much tonight." His wife said: "Now, wait just a minute, darling. I kept them up just as long as I could. Then I sent them up to their quarters, but I told them to sing just as long as they wanted to sing, and maybe you would get here soon. They couldn't go to sleep anyway, they were so excited. They're singing now, listen."

As they heard the strains of "Silent Night," he bounded up the steps and into the room with them. Then with a shout and a yell and a squeal, they jumped out of their beds. He sat down in the middle of the floor, and they all piled on top of him as they chatted and sang together. By-and-by the little girl, with her arm around his neck, said, "Daddy, is Santa Claus as sweet as you?" The telephone rang just a little while after that, and the nurse at the hospital said: "Doctor, I certainly hate to call you. I know you're dead tired, but there's an emergency here. It's a charity case." He said, "I'll be there in five minutes." He went on back to the hospital whistling, fresh and alert. As the nurse met him, she repeated, "Doctor, I'm sorry it's a charity case." He said, "Not for me it isn't." She said: "Oh, yes it is. They can't pay you anything." He said, "I've already been paid." So sometimes God sends spiritual food and strength by the most unexpected carriers.

Sometimes God answers this prayer for daily spiritual bread through the channel that Jesus used so often—secret prayer. He went into the garden of Gethsemane with his disciples, "And saith unto them, My soul is exceeding sorrowful unto death: tarry ye here, and watch. And he went forward a little, and fell on the ground, and prayed" (Mark 14:34–35). We have all marveled at his calmness and poise from that hour on to the end of the torment on the cross.

We so need to keep this channel open by starting the day alone with God. Then close the day with him. The prayer of Jesus for daily bread is a morning prayer and was never meant to be used once a month or even once a week. It is daily bread we need. We cannot feed our bodies once a week and expect to grow. Neither can we feed our souls spiritual food once a week and ever expect to grow in grace and likeness of our Saviour.

Someone asked a very lovely Christian, "What is the secret of your home being so happy and the adoration of your husband?" "It's very simple," she replied. "I'm nice to him three times a day. In the morning I walk with him to the car and find some way to show him I love and admire him. When he comes home in the evening, I go out to meet him with a smile and a welcome. At night we kneel together and pray." That is a wonderful recipe for keeping a relationship beautiful. Lift it a moment into the spiritual realm. Do we give our Heavenly Father enough of our time and attention? Do we put him first always?

3 Sometimes God sends us spiritual refreshments as the result of some task well done. In a way it is like the farmer working for the harvest. Several of the beautiful parables of Jesus deal with a vineyard, and the men who worked in them enjoyed some of the fruits. Each of these parables is used as an illustration of the spiritual kingdom. Our spiritual food comes as the harvest of spiritual work.

4 I called some time ago on a fine seventy-seven-year-old gentleman on his birthday. He was a Christian of the highest magnitude, and I said to him, "Tell me, as you look back across seventy-seven years, what do you remember with the most happiness?" He said: "That's right on my mind. See that big, comfortable chair right here? It looks very expensive to me. It's a birthday present. Years ago I found a man who had been whipped by drink. His life was a wreck. I led him to Christ. He and Christ and I overcame his weakness. He is an optometrist, and one day he came very humbly and very shamefacedly to ask if I would let him use my credit to get his office open again and to get his lights and water turned on. I offered to lend him some money, but he said, 'No, just let me use your name; just endorse it for me; let me use your

74

credit.' He paid it all back. That was nearly fifty years ago. Ever since then on my birthday and at Christmas he buys me some beautiful, expensive gift. He is very well-to-do now, but the thing that has brought me the most joy is to go past his place and realize that I had a part in that, and for him to come by every once in a while to see if I need anything and just to see if everything is all right. He tells me to call him any time I can think of something I want. He won't let me forget that his heart is full of gratitude. His prayers for me stay in my mind for days."

Dear Lord, give us each day some spiritual food for our souls. Help us not to fill up our lives with good things to the exclusion of the best. Amen.

For I was an hungred, and ye gave me no meat: I was thirsty, and ye gave me no drink: I was a stranger, and ye took me not in: naked, and ye clothed me not: sick, and in prison, and ye visited me not. Then shall they also answer him, saying, Lord, when saw we thee an hungred, or athirst, or a stranger, or naked, or sick, or in prison, and did not minister unto thee? Then shall he answer them, saying, Verily I say unto you, Inasmuch as ye did it not to one of the least of these, ye did it not to me. And these shall go away into everlasting punishment: but the righteous into life eternal.

MATTHEW 25:42–46

9

These Respectable Sins

A football player who was named "All American" on almost every sports writer's card and who graduated to pro football the following year wrote an article that was copied across the country. The title of the article was "God Keeps the Score." The player is a dedicated Christian. He was loved by all of his teammates for his clean living and his sense of fair play. The theme of his article was that the score on the scoreboard was not the most important thing. To him it was more important that he should play the game well and not do anything that would displease his Heavenly Father. The applause of the grandstand was always second to the applause of God. He had changed one word in the song that he loved, and instead of singing, "The eyes of Texas are upon you," he sang, "The eyes of Jesus are upon you."

What a contrast there is between his ideology and that of the Pharisees who lived in Jesus' time. Jesus accused them of saying long prayers in public places and of wearing phylacteries to be seen of men. They tried to obey all of the more than six hundred laws literally. To the common people of the day they were the most respected persons on earth. Therefore, it must have been a terrible shock to the disciples of

Jesus when he said to them, "Except your righteousness shall exceed the righteousness of the scribes and the Pharisees, ye shall in no wise enter into the kingdom of heaven." Jesus called the Pharisees hypocrites and told them they were as "whited sepulchres"—beautiful on the outside, very respectable, but ugly on the inside. He accused them of keeping the outside of the platter clean but of never washing the inside of the cup.

If Jesus stood in the pulpit of one of our big churches today and looked over the congregation, I doubt if he would find a single Pharisee. On the other hand, he might find many people who have never been guilty of committing a dishonorable or a disrespectable sin but who, like the Pharisees, are not pleasing to God. There are so many things that we may do or leave undone that will not affect our standing in the community or make us lose the respect of our fellowmen but which are sins in the eyes of God. Maybe it will not be right to call them "respectable" sins, for most certainly they are not respectable in the mind of Jesus. I invite you to look more closely at three of these sins.

The first one, in the words of Dr. Roy McClain, the splendid preacher of Atlanta, is the sin of *silence*. In his recent book *This Way, Please* is a thoughtful chapter entitled "The Sin of Silence." Let me quote a page from it.

It was said of the German General Von Moltke that "he could be silent in seven languages." It does look as though Christians could be vocal in at least one! In the midst of a desperate famine four Syrian lepers decided to fall into the hands of the enemy in order to keep from starving. Expecting arrest at any moment, they sauntered through the enemy camp grabbing bits of food wherever they could find them. But to their dismay no soldiers were near the camp, so the lepers sat down and gorged themselves into satisfaction. While they sat dozing from overeating, they remembered their families who were back home, consumed with hunger. This incident is recorded in the seventh chapter of II Kings where the spokesman finally admits, "We do not well: this day is a day of good tidings, and we hold our peace: If we tarry till the morning light, some mischief will come upon us. . . ." Equal guilt must be shared by the Christian church in the midpoint of this century because we do not well; this is the day of good tidings, and we hold our peace. For nearly two thousand years we have known the good news of salvation, yet enjoying it for ourselves, we have failed to propagate it. But inability to transmit news is not our problem. When a former President of the United States died, the news of his death was known around the world in less than thirty minutes.

The fact that the church is committing the sin of silence is apparent everywhere. For instance, in one of the major evangelical denominations it takes the efforts of thirty-one church members to win one other person to Christ in a year's time. In some of the "nonevangelical" groups that ratio is increased by forty to one. And yet this is the one thing that all professed Christians are called to do. Seeing is for the purpose of telling. If the experience with Jesus Christ is not of sufficient import to recommend it to someone else, then the whole structure of the kingdom is in question.

Events took a happier turn in the case of the Syrian lepers. At a certain point of saturation they decided, "Some greater mischief may befall us if we tarry until morning." The same probability, though with horrendous dimensions, may befall us because of our tarrying at the job. Among two and a half billion people, better than half that number are under communistic domination. *In 1904 one man kept preaching an infamous sermon, a sermon that produced seventeen converts. By 1917 these seventeen had become forty thousand. By 1933 their fold had swollen into the millions, insomuch that in 1955 there were nine hundred million plus!*

Why do we take our wonderful Christianity so lightly?

79

Since I have been in Miami, I have received a severe repri-
mand from a policeman. I deserved every word he said, although I hadn't done a thing except keep silent. A fine young
Christian and I were driving up an avenue when out of a
side street there shot a car which hit the car in front of us
and almost turned it over. I said to my companion: "Let's
get away from here. If we don't, they will be summoning us
to be witnesses in court, and it will take a day of our time."
So we turned into a side street and drove on to his place of
business. When I stopped the car, he didn't get out. After a
moment he said, "Are you thinking what I'm thinking?" I
said: "Yes, let's go back. That fellow who got hit will need
our testimony."

Sure enough, when we got back, the man whose car had
been struck was inarticulate, and the other man had about
convinced the policeman that it was not his fault. We pushed
through the crowd and told the policeman that we had witnessed what had happened. He laid his hand on my shoulder
pretty firmly and said, "Where have you been for the last ten
minutes?" I explained to him that I had driven away because
I didn't want to get mixed up in a court trial. He literally
blistered me, and I can still remember some of the things he
said: "There ought to be a law that would make it punishable
for anyone to do a thing like you have done. You live in a
country that boasts of justice, and then, because it will be a
little trouble to you, you run away and keep your mouth
shut."

Of course, there is no law that prevents anyone from committing this respectable sin. You can watch a man's house
burn down; you can stand there with your arms folded and
not turn in the alarm and still be a law-abiding citizen. You
can know that right next door to where you work or where

you live there is someone whose life is going to wreck, and you can do like Pilate did, wash your hands of the whole matter, and not be condemned as guilty by your fellow citizens. You can be in a crowd where someone ridicules Christianity or says vicious things about one of your closest friends, and you can keep silent and still be respected. But this we should remember, that God will not hold him guiltless who commits the sin of silence.

The second one is the sin of *lethargy*. Jesus scored this sin most severely, not once but many times. One of the longest stories that Jesus told was the story of the rich man and Lazarus. The rich man passed Lazarus every day. He drove out of his gates in his beautiful chariot with its golden harness and silver mountings and paid no attention at all to the hungry, suffering beggar at his gate. No one expected him to do otherwise. He lost no standing and no prestige and no face among his fellow men. Jesus never accused him of mistreating Lazarus. He didn't drive him away. He certainly didn't have him whipped. He just left him alone. Nobody blamed him. How succinctly this is expressed in the poem:

"When Jesus came to Golgotha they hanged Him on a tree,
  They drove great nails through hands and feet, and made
    a Calvary;
  They crowned Him with a crown of thorns, red were His
    wounds and deep.
  For those were crude and cruel days, and human flesh was
    cheap.

When Jesus came to Birmingham, they simply passed Him
    by,
  They never hurt a hair of Him, they only let Him die;

81

For men had grown more tender, and they would not give
  Him pain,
They only just passed down the street, and left Him in the
  rain.

Still Jesus cried, 'Forgive them, for they know not what they
  do,'
And still it rained the winter rain that chilled Him through
  and through;
The crowds went home and left the streets without a soul to
  see,
And Jesus crouched against a wall and cried for Calvary." *

Likewise, in the story of the good Samaritan the Levite and the priest lost no prestige as they passed by on the other side. In the line of duty, as far as they were concerned, this was no obligation of theirs. They had other important things which were their responsibilities. Nobody had assigned them the task of helping a man in trouble. They could hold their heads up and shrug their shoulders and keep the respect of others. But in neither of these two incidents were their records clean in the eyes of God. These men were sinners, and Jesus made it very, very plain when he came to the end of the story of Lazarus that the sins which are so easily condoned by our fellow men are not overlooked by God, who loves us and wants us to be like his Son.

This particular truth was so important to Jesus that he gave us two other parables about it—the parable of the talents and the parable of the pounds. Whenever through the years I have thought of the return of that man who was given one talent, I have pictured him smiling smugly as he took out his one

---

* G. A. Studdert-Kennedy, "Indifference," *The Sorrows of God* (New York: Harper & Brothers, 1924). Used by permission.

talent, unwrapped the napkin, brushed off the dirt, and laid the talent before the master. He had an idea that he was a wonderfully honest man. He hadn't stolen any part of the talent. He hadn't lost any part of it. I imagine he was very much surprised when his master condemned him and asked him a searching question about why he had not used his talent. Jesus told us in another unforgettable passage that there are going to be many people surprised when they stand before the judgment bar of God, because they have left undone so many things they should have done. "Inasmuch as ye did it not to one of the least of these, ye did it not to me. And these shall go away into everlasting punishment."

Many years ago at Ridgecrest I heard Charles Wells, the world correspondent for a big syndicate of newspapers, relate an interesting incident. He was in China before the war and was awakened by some shots under his hotel window. When he dared to risk looking out, he saw four Chinese men lying on the pavement in front of a billboard. They had been shot while trying to tear down a poster which had been put up during the night by Communists. The poster pictured four strong men, all different nationalities, holding the staff of a large Communist flag which stood out in the breeze. They were standing shoulder to shoulder and represented unity of purpose. Underneath were the words, "Black man, brown man, yellow man, Communist, together we can conquer the world." Charles Wells' application was a masterpiece. "Why haven't we placarded the world with posters picturing a Christian flag floating above four strong men and underneath it the caption, 'Black man, brown man, yellow man, Christian, together we can conquer the world with the glorious truths and principles of Jesus'? Together we can conquer war, pestilence, and evil."

Another "respectable" sin is that of *robbing God*. The first reaction of many of us would be exactly the same as that of those men to whom Malachi was speaking when he said, "Ye have robbed God." Their question was, "Wherein have we robbed God?" Malachi's answer came back like a shot, "In tithes and offerings, that's where you have robbed God." This particular sin is very, very prevalent in every church. Alas, it is committed by most of the people of every church. I read just the other day that across America less than 20 per cent of the people in any given church are contributing over 90 per cent of all the budget of their churches. One day Jesus sat by the treasury and watched those silken-clad, rich, respectable, esteemed, honored Pharisees walk up and proudly lay their offerings on the table. Not a word of commendation did he say. Then one little widow came and gave a tiny gift, just two mites, and Jesus said, "Of a truth I say unto you, that this poor widow hath cast in more than they all."

I read a story not long ago that sums up these "respectable" sins better than any words that I could use. A schoolteacher was telling about a personable little boy named Ronnie, who was very lovable and always a perfect little gentleman. He made splendid grades in his daily work but became highly nervous and tense when a test was given. One particular day after she had written the arithmetic problems for the test on the blackboard, she went back to her desk. A few moments later she thought of Ronnie and looked over at him. Sure enough, his chin was quivering and tears were not far away. She got up and walked to the back of the room and then came down the aisle and stopped behind him. It took just a glance to see the mistakes he had made. She sat down by him and, nudging him with her elbow, said, "Ronnie, did you add this?" His face reddened a little as he said, "Oh, I forgot."

84

She looked at the next one, put her finger on a figure, and said, "Ronnie, did you subtract this one?" Without a word, he corrected it. Then as she nudged him again and got up to leave, she said, "Ronnie, don't forget to divide the next one." She went back to her chair, and from somewhere came the thought: "My life is a little like Ronnie's test paper. I forgot to add to it some of the things that my Master wanted me to do. I haven't subtracted some of the resentments that I should have gotten rid of a long time ago. I haven't divided with my Lord my abilities, my talents, and my time." She added, "My chin began to quiver, too, and the tears were not far away."

How well this story illustrates some of these things which we call respectable sins but which God calls just sins.

Gracious Father, forgive us, and as David prayed, "Cleanse us from our secret sins and unite our hearts to fear thy name." We would be good, Father. Guide our erring feet. We ask it in Jesus' name. Amen.

For with the heart man believeth unto righteousness; and with the mouth confession is made unto salvation. For the scripture saith, Whosoever believeth on him shall not be ashamed. For there is no difference between the Jew and the Greek: for the same Lord over all is rich unto all that call upon him. For whosoever shall call upon the name of the Lord shall be saved. How then shall they call on him in whom they have not believed? and how shall they believe in him of whom they have not heard? and how shall they hear without a preacher? And how shall they preach, except they be sent? as it is written, How beautiful are the feet of them that preach the gospel of peace, and bring glad tidings of good things!

ROMANS 10:10–15

10

The Lord Is Rich

Dr. W. C. Speakman for many years was a leader in evangelism and missionary zeal in his denomination. When asked by a friend what inspired him to be so zealous, his answer was about like this. "One day as I walked up to the entrance of a department store, the big glass doors flew open before I touched them. I was so startled that I just stood with my mouth open and looked to the right and to the left to see who had opened them. There was no one anywhere near me, and involuntarily I stepped back, and, lo and behold, the doors closed. Bewildered, I came to the conclusion that it was some trick or prank that was being played on me. Then I heard footsteps behind me, and a little lady passed, going right up to those doors. She didn't even lift her hand, as I had done, to open them. Once again the doors flew open and, without being the least perturbed, she walked on through and the doors closed behind her. I gingerly took another step forward, and when they opened, I entered the store. Then I made some discreet inquiries, and I learned that the doors were controlled by an electric beam. When anyone broke the beam, the doors automatically opened.

"After I got back to my study, it suddenly dawned on me

that it wouldn't make any difference who walked up to those doors, they would open. It wouldn't matter of what nationality or race or color they were, or whether it was a woman or a man or a child, the doors would open. Then with a thrill I realized what a perfect illustration this was of God's impartiality. The words of Paul burst on my mind, 'God is no respecter of persons,' and I arrived at the great astounding truth that 'whosoever will' may walk up to the doors of the kingdom of heaven, and they will fly open and he can go in and find salvation and peace of mind."

How beautifully the story illustrates the words of Paul in the tenth chapter of Romans, "For there is no difference between the Jew and the Greek: for the same Lord over all is rich unto all that call upon him." There is a joyous note in the voice of Paul in this tenth chapter. He was excited and exuberant because God had singled him out to take a particularly great message to the whole world. God had pushed back the horizons. God had given him wings. He had a vision of taking the glad tidings to the ends of the earth. He would go to Rome, to Spain, to the uttermost parts of the globe.

A young missionary from Africa, on her first furlough, was giving her testimony in prayer meeting at her home church. She said, "I have been asked to tell when I first felt the call to go to Africa as a missionary." She lifted her eyes and looked around at the beautiful auditorium and said: "It was when this church building was completed. On the Saturday before our first worship service here I came up to fix the flowers. In front of the church a little Negro boy was standing on the sidewalk, with his eyes as big as marbles, looking in awe and amazement at this huge church building. I stopped and watched him for a minute and then said, 'Isn't it beautiful?' He looked at me and then back at the church and then silently nodded his head in the affirmative. I invited him to come and look inside. We walked up the steps together and entered the big front door. He stopped and slowly turned his head from side to side, then looked up at the tall ceiling and back at the great organ. I asked him, 'What do you think of it?' His answer made my heart cry. In a very low voice he said, 'Is it just for white people?' I never got over the wistfulness in that little boy's voice. It hurt me away down deep to have to tell him that *this church* was just for white people, but I hastened on to tell him that the gospel of Jesus was for *all people*. From there it was just a step for me to understand that God needed me to take his gospel of salvation to others."

The glad tidings would not be limited to the sublime fact that a Saviour is born. Paul's message was bigger than the wonderful news that people could be saved from their sins. Salvation they could have, and more. They could become the children of a Father who was rich. His wealth could not be counted. He was rich in everything, and his riches would be theirs, for "the same Lord over all is rich unto all that call upon him." Paul had tasted a little of God's wealth of power on that road to Damascus; and he glimpsed his wealth of knowledge and wisdom when he was rescued from enemies who had plotted to kill him. Even dungeons and chains were nothing to God. A big part of Paul's message revolved around the truth that God was rich in all spheres of life. Look more closely at four of God's riches which mean so much to us.

He is rich in *material things*. While this is not the central theme that Paul is presenting here, we should never forget the word written down in the Old Testament: "The cattle of a thousand hills belong to him. The gold and the silver are his." We should never forget that this is God's world, that he created it, owns it, and is sovereign in it. Jesus made this so plain in many of his parables. We get so intensely interested in what the men did with those talents that Jesus spoke of that we forget the opening sentence telling that the owner *gave* them the talents. They belonged to him. He expected them to use those talents, and he fully expected a return. We are tenants and stewards of God's wealth. We are "strangers and sojourners." The material things belong to God, and he does bless us, as he promised in the third chapter of Malachi, with an outpouring of material things as well as spiritual things.

One day I was speaking in a former pastorate on "The Unsearchable Riches of God," and I made the statement that these riches of which Paul spoke were not material riches but spiritual riches. After the sermon a lawyer friend of twenty years' standing came up and put a hand on each of my shoulders. He put his face up close to mine and said: "Roy, don't ever make that mistake again. Don't ever say that God doesn't pour out upon us material riches when we prove our good stewardship. Come down to my office in the morning. I have something to show you." The next morning I walked into one of the finest suites of offices I ever saw. It was elegantly appointed and furnished. He escorted me through the ten or twelve rooms and introduced me to his associates and partners. When we came back to his private office, he asked: "Do you remember what my office was like when you left here? Do you remember that it consisted of one shabby room, no carpet on the floor, and an old battered desk? I did not even have a secretary. Many times I have said this to others, and I say it now to you: 'God gave me this prosperity. God made me immensely wealthy. God did it, and if you want to look at my books, you will see that I don't give him a tenth—I give him one half.' So I repeat what I said last night, 'Don't ever say that God's riches are confined to spiritual things.' " So I say here with assurance, God *is* rich in material things.

God is rich in *happiness*. I am sure this was one of the things that Paul definitely had in mind. There was a phrase that was on his lips continually, "Rejoice in the Lord alway: and again I say, Rejoice." He was forever talking about the joy that God gave. I sometimes think he took as the text of all of his letters the words of Jesus, "I came that you might have life and might have it more abundantly."

I recently read a delightful illustration of this. Bishop Cavanaugh, of the Methodist Church, in one of his early pastorates teamed up with a physician to do personal work. The two of them became a powerful factor for good not only in his church, but in the whole city. They lifted the spiritual level of their town to a new high. One day someone asked the bishop how it came about. His answer was something like this: "When I came to this pastorate, I met the physician, who was a skeptic. Our paths crossed time after time, and we became friends. One day as I was walking down the street, the physician pulled his buggy up to the curb and asked me to ride with him, for he wanted to talk to me. Our conversation started like this: 'Preacher, you and I are good friends, and I wouldn't offend you for anything, but you puzzle me. How in this world can a man of your intellectual ability spend his life telling this "old wives' tale" of God's love and his power and the resurrection of Jesus?' This was the opening I had waited for, and I sent a prayer to God before I answered slowly: 'Doctor, suppose in your younger days you had a cancer and there came to you a man who told you that he had a prescription that had cured many cancers and he wanted you

91

to try it. Suppose you had accepted it and used it and it had cured you. What would the world think of you if you would not take that same prescription to every patient of yours who had a cancer?' Quick as a flash he answered, 'They would say I was a fool.' I looked him earnestly in the face and said: 'Doctor, twenty-five years ago I had a cancer—not the kind with which you deal. You could call mine a moral cancer, and the Great Physician gave me a prescription that cured me. What would you think of me, Doctor, if I didn't take that prescription to every single person that I could possibly reach who needed it—every single one that has some great heartache or some sin that needs wiping out? I repeat, what would you think of me?' After a long silence he answered: 'Guess I would have to say the same thing. You would be a fool.' We stopped the buggy in a quiet place, and I poured out my soul to him. Finally, he accepted Jesus Christ as Saviour. We teamed up to take this particular kind of riches, which Christ has to offer, to everyone we could find. The doctor and I cured the soul sickness of many, many people and had a glorious good time doing it. I think we were the two happiest men in that city."

That is the kind of riches that I am sure Paul was talking about when he said, "My Lord is rich unto all that call upon him." I don't see how you and I can get away from that doctor's words when he answered the bishop's question. Jesus was particularly hard on the man who wrapped up his talent in a napkin and buried it. Christianity moves ahead so slowly because we do not individually witness more effectively for him. So many others have found happiness and abundant living in doing exactly what Paul and the doctor and the bishop did. God doesn't need only preachers to preach the gospel and people who have beautiful voices to sing the gospel, but he also needs every one of us in our workaday clothes to be his witnesses. He needs the rank and file of all who have accepted the same prescription and have found the power of Jesus Christ helpful in the things that would wreck and ruin their lives. He needs every one of us to do exactly what Paul was so joyfully doing.

God is rich in *mercy*. As the psalmist said, "His mercy endureth forever." The most welcome truth in the whole Bible to every one of us is that God forgives and that when he forgives he forgets. "Though your sins be as scarlet, they shall be as white as snow."

An old Saxon king gathered his troops together to put down a rebellion, led by a wicked rascal. The battle was short and decisive. The king's army was victorious. Then the old Saxon, who was a Christian, sent messages throughout the realm to proclaim to all: "The king is in his army tent, and in front of it is a big torch. As long as the torch burns, every man who was in the rebellion can have a full pardon by going to the king and asking forgiveness. When the torch burns out, it will be too late."

We, too, can have forgiveness if we come humbly to God and ask. "Ask, and it shall be given you; seek, and ye shall find; knock, and it shall be opened unto you." How pathetic it is that some will put off this coming until their hearts are so hardened that it is too late. Even though God is rich in mercy, they remain lost.

God is rich in *power to transform our lives*. I sometimes think the greatest miracles that were ever performed by Jesus Christ were not the miracles recorded in the New Testament. We marvel at the stilling of the storm, the feeding of the five thousand and the healing of the lepers. Those were wonderful days! The disciples were thrilled at what they saw

93

their Master do. To me, none of these are as wonderful as the transformation that Jesus has brought about in the lives of people whom I have known. To say that God is rich in his power to transform ugly lives into wonderful lives is an understatement. Think of this one.

In a town in the Middle West a Methodist church needed a sexton. The Reverend Baxter called his stewards together and suggested that they employ a ne'er-do-well by the name of Anderson. There was silence for a while in the board of stewards, and then someone asked: "Is that the best we can do? He has been a bum for years. No one in the city has any respect for him." So they decided to wait another week and try to find someone else. Finally, in desperation they employed him. As the months went by and he took pride in his work, they noticed a definite change in him. He kept his clothes clean, and he kept the church clean. He became more and more polite, agreeable, and anxious to please. For a year he sat on the back seat at every service and was one of the most attentive listeners in the congregation. Then one day he went over to Dr. Baxter's home and asked if he could join the church. He answered all of the preacher's questions in a most satisfactory way, and they accepted him into the church.

Another year passed, and again he came to Dr. Baxter, this time to ask if they would trust him to teach a class of boys. He was still teaching this class of boys when Dr. Baxter left for another pastorate. It was ten years before he came back to that town. A number of his old stewards met him at the train. After the greetings, with a twinkle in his eye, the chairman of the board said: "Dr. Baxter, I will drive you over to the home where you are to be a guest, for your host could not get away from a meeting of the board of directors of the First National Bank. You are to stay at the home of

Mr. Anderson." When a puzzled look came over the preacher's face, the whole group laughed aloud. Then the chairman told Dr. Baxter what had happened: "Mr. Anderson is now the most popular and respected man in the city. He is president of the First National Bank. A wealthy uncle discovered the transformation that had come over his nephew and left him a fortune in his will. He still teaches a class of boys in Sunday school, and he is still the sexton of the church. Over and over he has said, 'God cleaned my life and my very soul, and as long as I live, I will personally see that his house is kept clean.' You are to stay in the most luxurious home in our city."

Paul was so right when he said, "God is rich in everything."

"My father is rich in houses and lands,
He holdeth the wealth of the world in His hands!
Of rubies and diamonds, of silver and gold,
His coffers are full, He has riches untold.

I'm a child of the King, a child of the King:
With Jesus my Saviour, I'm a child of the King.

My Father's own Son, the Saviour of men,
Once wandered on earth as the poorest of them;
But now He is pleading our pardon on high,
That we may be His when He comes by and by.

I once was an outcast stranger on earth,
A sinner by choice, and an alien by birth
But I've been adopted, my name's written down,
An heir to a mansion, a robe, and a crown."

Our Father, grant us the realization that you have done and will do above all that we could ask or think. Help us to live lives of gratitude. Amen.

95

Then the eleven disciples went away into Galilee, into a mountain where Jesus had appointed them. And when they saw him, they worshipped him: but some doubted. And Jesus came and spake unto them, saying, All power is given unto me in heaven and in earth. Go ye therefore, and teach all nations, baptizing them in the name of the Father, and of the Son, and of the Holy Ghost: Teaching them to observe all things whatsoever I have commanded you: and, lo, I am with you alway, even unto the end of the world. Amen.

MATTHEW 28:16–20

11

To All Nations

The favorite story of Dr. Gonzalez, one of the great preachers, was: "When God was creating the world, there came to him one day four angels, each one with a question. The first one asked, 'How are you creating the world?' The second asked, 'Why?' The third one, 'May I have it when you finish?' The fourth one's question was, 'Can I help?' " Dr. Gonzalez said, "The first angel asked the scientist's question, and it's a good question. Through all these years the scientists and the physicists have bent over their test tubes searching for the 'how.' The second is the philosopher's question. It, too, is a good question, and it is not confined to the university professors of philosophy, for into the minds of every one of us comes the puzzling question, 'Why did God create us and our world?' The third, 'May I have it?' is the epitome of selfishness. We are ashamed of that question, and yet so many of us spend a whole lifetime building a fence around a little part of this good earth, and some nations are trying persistently to get control and rule the whole world. It's an ugly question. The fourth one, 'Can I help?' is the Christian's question. It was born in the Spirit of Jesus. We hear Paul in awe and conviction whispering, 'Lord, what wilt thou have me to do?' "

This story is a beautiful introduction to the twenty-eighth chapter of Matthew. Jesus had finished his course. He was speaking his last words to his disciples. He, too, had created something wonderful and new, the kingdom of God on earth. There was just one final command to be given. A little group of eleven men stood on a mountain in Galilee. I think they had only one question in their minds. It was the Christian's question, "Can we help?" Jesus answered it without it being asked, "Go ye and teach all nations." Not another word needed to be said. After these nineteen hundred years we read the sentence that Jesus spoke to them, and if we really belong to him, uppermost in our minds and hearts will be the same question, "Can I help?" These eleven men who stood around Jesus before his ascension were so filled and surcharged with the power, the personality, the Spirit of Jesus that the only thing in their minds was: "What do you want us to do? Where do we go? How can we help? Just point the direction." I have an idea they were so thrilled by what they had seen and what they had heard that they could hardly wait in Jerusalem to be endued with the Holy Spirit.

It was as Dr. S. D. Gordon said at Ridgecrest one day, "If you are not interested in sending the story of Jesus Christ everywhere around this world, and everywhere around you, then you had better examine yourself, because the chances are that Christ does not mean very much to you." For ten minutes he talked on in the same vein: "If you are not active, if you are not doing something about sending or taking the message of Jesus to other people, there is something wrong in your relationship to God. Jesus talked about the kingdom in terms of meat and bread and water, the great necessities of life."

Dr. Gordon paused a moment and then continued: "I had

a dream one night that I wish every Christian could have. I dreamed that I had come into my pulpit one Sunday morning a moment or two before the services and sat down in the big chair reserved for me. Then I noticed coming down the center aisle a stranger. There was something unusual and attractive about him. He was plainly dressed, but there was nothing plain about his countenance. He walked quietly to the front and turned into a rented pew of one of my good friends. When my friend looked up at him, surprise and delight were written all over his face. He reached out both hands to welcome him. I made up my mind that as soon as the service was over I would get down there and meet him. So after the benediction I pushed through the crowd at the front and finally got to the pew, but he was gone. 'Who was your friend?' I asked of the owner of the pew. In surprise he answered, 'Didn't you know him, Dr. Gordon?' I said, 'No, I didn't.' 'Why,' he said, 'it was Christ Jesus. He came to worship with us. He has been here many times before.' "

Dr. Gordon said: "When I awoke, I was trembling and in a cold sweat. Frantically, I was trying to remember what my sermon was about. What had I said? Did I preach the gospel in such a way that the Master was happy? Was I giving him all the credit, or was I tacking the name of Gordon up here and there to be praised by men? There was no more sleep for me that night. I examined myself. For the rest of my pastorate there I never sat down in that pulpit chair without thinking or praying: 'Jesus, if you are here, listen carefully. I will be talking about you. I will be trying to carry out the Great Commission, to take your story and your message to my little part of the world. I will be careful not to take any of the praise nor try to impress anyone with my personality. I am preaching for you.' "

As I sat there listening to Dr. Gordon that day, I was reminded of those disciples who didn't care what happened to them or what people did to them or thought about them, they were going to tell the story of Jesus Christ to every ear that would listen—in jail, in prison, before the human judges, wherever they could get a hearing. "To all nations" was still ringing in their ears, and to all nations they went. There are so many reasons for us to help carry out that Commission. Let me mention two.

The first reason that we should take the gospel to all nations is the universal hunger in the hearts of all people to know God better and to have spiritual security.

Dr. G. Whitfield Guinness, one of the great missionaries of the last century, said: "There was a community close to my station that I wanted above everywhere else to enter and preach the gospel. It was in Nepal. [This is an independent kingdom in the Himalayas.] They would let no missionary in. I tried every way to get admission but was refused. Once I slipped in, and they caught me and escorted me out. My persistence didn't end, and I finally was allowed to enter under the conditions that I would promise not to carry a Bible or preach anywhere or mention to anyone the name of Jesus Christ. I found Nepal a perfectly beautiful valley, lovely in every way. On one side was a big snow-covered mountain. On top of that mountain there was a lake on which the ice melted for one short period of each year. In the bottom of that lake you could see through the clear, sparkling water a stone idol, an image of the god they thought controlled the doors to heaven. Anyone who climbed that snow-covered mountain and looked down into the deep lake and saw clearly the image of their god was assured of eternity. Every summer when the ice melted, men closed their stores and their shops and their businesses and climbed the mountain. They carried the sick and the afflicted up that steep incline. Thousands of them died on the dangerous trek. Why? Because they wanted to make sure that their souls would be saved forever."

Dr. Guinness, speaking here in our country, said in substance: "The people of Nepal are far hungrier for salvation than the people of America. All around us there are literally thousands of people here in America who pay no attention whatsoever to whether their souls are going to be saved hereafter or whether they are saved now, and they care less about the people on the other side of the world. They let them die in their ignorance when we have the story and the answer because we have Jesus Christ. Never in Nepal has been sung, 'What a friend we have in Jesus, all our sins and griefs to bear,' and the reason is so pathetic. We have never accepted for ourselves the challenge of the Master, 'Go ye therefore and teach all nations.' "

The second reason for witnessing is the need of the people for that which Jesus only can give. Jesus made it so plain with his proclamation in his home city, Nazareth, the day he stood up to read in the synagogue. Deliberately he did a daring thing. He read from the sixty-first chapter of the prophecy of Isaiah, "The Spirit of the Lord is upon me, because he hath anointed me to preach the gospel to the poor; he hath sent me to heal the brokenhearted, to preach deliverance to the captives, and recovering of sight to the blind, to set at liberty them that are bruised, to preach the acceptable year of the Lord." Luke records only a part of two verses, but Jesus probably read much more. The very next verse in Isaiah sums up the things the Messiah would do: "To give unto them beauty for ashes, the oil of joy for mourning, the garment of praise for the spirit of heaviness." So the Master's mission was not only to save us from our sins and assure us of eternity with God but also to make life here on this earth wonderful and full: "To give unto them beauty for ashes, the oil of joy for mourning . . ." Our missionaries have blazed a trail through the dark areas of the world. Their prime mission has been to teach people about God as revealed through Jesus, to give them peace of mind and spirit, to throw open the gates of heaven. Modern medicine and the blessings of finer living have gone down that trail with them or close behind them. Physical suffering has fallen back before the firm tread of our missionaries.

Several years ago the editor of *The Saturday Evening Post* said to one of his best reporters: "A lot is being written about foreign missions. I want you to get some facts that will justify the foreign mission program or not justify it. For me, I don't care which it is, but I want a realistic story." The reporter discovered that the Reverend Deems, a very famous evangelistic missionary, had recently returned from Africa. So he found Dr. Deems and made an appointment with him. He wanted to put the missionary on the defensive, so he began: "Dr. Deems, I'm a writer. I guess you would call me a reporter. I'm looking for a story on foreign missions. I don't believe in foreign missions myself. I don't believe it is justified. I don't believe it is worth the expenditure and the sacrifice people make. Can you justify foreign missions so that a layman like me can understand it?"

Dr. Deems answered after a moment: "Yes, I can justify it, and I can defend it down on your level, not up on mine— on *your* level. You listen to this. I was going from the home station to one of the outstations to fill my regular appointment. I knew there would be a crowd waiting, so I was hurrying. As I went along the trail, I found a mother waiting for me. She was weeping. As she knelt down in the dust in front of me, she said: 'Oh, Dr. Deems, you just must come to my home. My seventeen-year-old daughter is very ill. Please, Dr. Deems, please come.' I asked, 'How far is it?' She said, 'Right there in the village, right over there.' I said, 'Well, you know I'm not a medical man, but I'll go with you, and if there is anything one of our doctors can do, I'll send for him.' When I arrived, I found the daughter with a great big, ugly hole in her chest. I asked, 'What in the world made that?' She said: 'Dr. Deems, we sent for the medicine man, and he listened to her chest. He told us that the growling was a demon inside of her.' Of course, I knew it was either pneumonia or bronchitis. They had heated a piece of iron white hot and bored a hole in the chest of that poor little helpless girl."

The writer for *The Saturday Evening Post* said: "By that time Dr. Deems was striding up and down the room with his fists clenched, eyes blazing, and he whirled around and fired at me: '*You* can understand that. *That's down where you live.* Do you still think it's not worthwhile to send a Saviour to these people to lift their whole lives up, not just for heaven and eternity, but for *here?* Can you understand that?'" The reporter answered: "Dr. Deems, please forgive me. I do believe in foreign missions. I was just trying to make you do exactly what you've done. I believe in missions. I'm a Christian. Thank you, Doctor, for some mighty facts that I can use." So he wrote the whole account for *The Saturday Evening Post*. When I finished reading that story in the *Post*, I decided I would clip it out and tell it wherever I found someone with a question about the worthwhileness of foreign missions. Not only does the message of Jesus mean salvation for those who would accept him, but it also means a sweeter and a happier life here. Christianity is not just something to take the sting out of death. It was given to us to take the stings out of life here on this good earth.

With these things in mind, I am sure that every one of us would want to say, "How can I help to take to all nations this thrilling story?" There are two things that are needed. First, God needs volunteers. God needs young men and young women who will dedicate their lives to the mission fields of the world. The need is for men and women like the eleven men that stood with Jesus on that mountaintop—men and women who will say with them, "Which way, Lord, and when do I start? Where do you want me to go?" He needs men and women who are not asking what the hardships are or what they will be expected to do but are willing to say:

"I'll go where You want me to go, dear Lord,
O'er mountain or plain or sea;
I'll say what You want me to say, dear Lord,
I'll be what You want me to be."

There is one meeting of the Foreign Mission Board in Richmond that none of us who were present will ever forget. Dr. Maddry was presiding at the examination of some young people who were ready to go to the foreign mission field. He began the examination by turning to us and making this statement: "Brethren, we are here to examine these who have met the requirements thus far for the foreign mission field. I think we will find before we have finished that we are not examining them but we are examining ourselves, and they are going to make us wonder whether we have as much of the Spirit of Jesus Christ in our hearts as they have." Then he presented the first candidate, a trained nurse. She was asked the usual questions. She answered them all perfectly. After a moment of silence Dr. Maddry said to her: "Do you realize that in China there are no operating rooms like the ones you have here in America? Do you realize that there will be more dirt in the hospital than you have ever seen? The floors, the pans, the instruments, and everything in the room will be dirty." Her eyes literally flashed as she answered, "They may be dirty when I get there, but they won't be dirty long." There was a silence for a full minute, then some of us reached for our handkerchiefs. Dr. Maddry was right. We wondered if we had that same kind of dedication. We needed to examine our own hearts.

Paul was logical when he asked, "How shall they hear without a preacher, and how shall they preach except they be sent?" There is no other way to send those who are called to go unless each of us reads the Great Commission as a personal order and a challenge. A glorious church will be a church with a glorious missionary zeal. God bless the women of our missionary societies who have so beautifully kept this mission zeal aflame in our churches. God bless the men who have not been called to go themselves but have so conscientiously given of their substance and their possessions that they might have a representative in some faraway land.

In North Carolina there was a deacon whose pastor called him in one day for a conference. In substance he said to the deacon: "There is a young man from one of our finest Christian homes who feels definitely the call to be a missionary. His family cannot afford to send him through college, so I am not going to mince words with you. I am going to level with you. You are wealthy. I think God wants you to see him through. Will you do it?" Without a moment's hesitation,

105

the answer came back, "Yes, sir, pastor, I'll do it." The pastor sat with his mouth hanging open in astonishment. The deacon began to chuckle. "You thought you were going to have to do some selling, didn't you? You thought you were going to have to use some pressure and some persuasion, didn't you? You weren't expecting me to say right off, 'Yes, I'll finance him through college and the seminary.' Well, let me tell you why I answered so fast. God is giving me a second chance. Fifteen years ago God sent the preacher to me with the same proposition, and I turned him down. That boy I didn't help is one of the grandest preachers today that I have ever heard, and I cry every time I hear him preach because I could be standing behind him in the pulpit wherever he goes, if I hadn't said no to God. Sure, I'll send your missionary. Who is he?" Now, listen to the pastor's answer, for it will give you a thrill. "Theron Rankin is the boy. Theron Rankin," he repeated. Theron Rankin spent years as a missionary in China and then became secretary of the Foreign Mission Board.

God does not give to many of us such a golden opportunity and such a deep, rewarding experience, but he does give to all of us a chance to have a part in sending men like Theron Rankin to teach all nations.

Dear Lord, give us eyes that can see the glorious opportunities to tell the old, old story to those around us. Give us clarity of vision to see our responsibility to have a part in sending Jesus to all nations. Amen.

Then said Jesus unto them, When ye have lifted up the Son of man, then ye shall know that I am he, and that I do nothing of myself; but as my Father hath taught me, I speak these things. And he that sent me is with me: the Father hath not left me alone; for I do always those things that please him. As he spake these words, many believed on him. Then said Jesus to those Jews which believed on him, If ye continue in my word, then are ye my disciples indeed; and ye shall know the truth, and the truth shall make you free.

JOHN 8:28–32

12

Truth and Freedom

An article appeared in a newspaper the day after Christmas. It was written in New York and said in substance: "Maybe the finest Christmas present that was received in this city went to a man who has been in Sing Sing for six years. He was serving a life sentence for a murder with which he had nothing to do. He was not guilty. He was released because a hardened old criminal with a long police record had a conscience. He was dying, and on his deathbed he confessed to the murder that had sent the innocent man to prison. The state of New York will probably pay the man they released yesterday twenty or twenty-five thousand dollars. It makes me wonder how many more men are in prison across the country who would be *set free if the truth were known.*"

You could hardly read that last sentence without recalling the words of Jesus, "Ye shall know the truth, and the truth shall make you free." Here are two big words, *truth* and *freedom,* that belong near to the heart of Christianity. Both of them were continually on the lips of Jesus and Paul and John. Both words antagonized the people of their day. When Jesus spoke the sentence mentioned, the Jews bristled up immediately and answered, "We be Abraham's seed, and were never in bondage to any man: how sayest thou, Ye shall be made free?"

And when Jesus used the word "truth" in his talk with Pilate, the Roman ended the conversation with a sneering question, "What is truth?" I imagine he would have been even more confused if Jesus had answered him as he did Thomas in the fourteenth chapter of John, "I am the truth." We can make some allowance for the misunderstanding of Jesus by the people of that day. But we can hardly make allowance for anyone who would misunderstand him today. A legion have testified that Jesus has set them free from their worst enemies.

Look briefly at three of these hurtful things from which the truth has set us free.

In the words of Paul, "Jesus hath made me free from the law of sin and death." Paul's heart was singing as he said: "I am no longer under the law. I am under a different dispensation. I am under grace." Did Paul mean to infer that if anyone accepted Jesus Christ as Lord and Saviour there would be no penalty exacted for the things he did that were wrong? No, not at all. Paul well knew that a man could accept Christ and be forgiven for his sins and still be sent to the penitentiary for punishment. Is he contradicting those well-known verses of Scripture which read, "The wages of sin is death," and "Whatsoever a man soweth that shall he also reap"? Again, the answer is no. The law of sin and death to which Paul refers means the death of the soul, and when you accept Jesus Christ as Saviour, all the sins that you have committed are blotted out of God's books and they are separated from you as far as the east is from the west. Paul was not even thinking of the penalties attached to breaking the natural laws of the universe. Neither was he thinking of man-made laws. Full

110

many a time we reap what we sow right here on earth, and full many a time the wages of sin is death to our ambitions, to the happiness of our homes, and to a multitude of other things. All of this was so small by the side of the death of the soul that he didn't even stop to explain. His heart was singing so that he wanted to shout from the housetop, "I am free from the law of sin and death."

Dr. Charlie Hewitt, who later became assistant pastor of the Temple Baptist Church in Philadelphia, was sent by a magazine editor to interview Dr. Russell Conwell. It was on Dr. Conwell's eighty-third birthday, and he was confined to his bed most of the time. Charlie said: "Dr. Conwell, our editor thinks the world would like to hear what you have to say on this, your eighty-third birthday. As you look back across your life, what stands out? Are you most thankful for any one experience or any one victory or achievement?" After a moment of silence Dr. Conwell answered: "I am very thankful and glad about many things. One, of course, is Temple University, but as big as that is, it's not equal in size to what happened to me in the army. A boy by the name of Johnny Ring was assigned to me as my orderly. Somehow, I became his hero. He anticipated my every wish and was as devoted as a son. In the night a surprise attack by the enemy drove us across a bridge. We immediately set the bridge on fire to retard their pursuit. Then I discovered that in my hurry I had left my sword in the tent. Without a word, Johnny Ring broke away from me and ran across that burning bridge and retrieved my sword. He received third-degree burns. The doctor looked at him and sadly shook his head. Nothing could be done for him.

"He not only saved my sword, but God used him to save my soul. I sat down beside his cot and watched him as he

111

twisted and tossed in agony. The question kept boiling up in my mind, 'Why, why, why did Johnny Ring give his life to save my sword?' Of course, the answer was that Johnny Ring loved me, unworthy as I was—and I was unworthy. It was just a step from there to the question that had made me a skeptic. 'Why did Christ die for a sinner?' I had never been able to understand or accept the atonement. Suddenly I saw it clearly. Christ, like Johnny Ring, suffered for the same reason—because he loved us. My doubts fled. Right then and there I accepted Christ and promised him that I would do the work of two, Johnny Ring and myself. I asked God to forgive me for the way I had lived and the way I had doubted. A great peace settled over me, and a wonderful new life opened in front of me."

How splendidly this illustrates the power of Jesus Christ to strike off our shackles and set us free.

"Ye shall know the truth, and the truth shall make you free"—from fear. Before we look at the teaching of Jesus about fear, we should remind ourselves that fear is an emotion with which the whole animal kingdom is born. It is necessary and good. It is not to be gotten rid of, but it is to be controlled and mastered. We rightly teach our children to fear fire, traffic, and many other things. Also, fear is a spur that can shoot an extra dose of adrenalin into our blood stream and add power to our muscles.

I like the tall tale a Texan tells. While it is exaggerated, it surely illustrates this truth. He was telling a crowd of Easterners about the viciousness of the wild steers on the range. "I was walking along close to a mesquite thicket the other day when one of these critters crashed out and came for me. I ran for the closest tree. The lowest branch on it was twenty feet up. There was nothing to do but to jump for it."

112

There the Texan paused and reached for his tobacco and started rolling a cigarette. The tense silence was broken by an anxious voice, "Did you catch it?" The Texan drawled, "No, I missed it going up, but I caught it coming down."

Fear is an emotion of high voltage and can be an ally or an enemy. It should be mastered and controlled or we will wreck our lives with worry and anxiety about the things that never happen or are best for us if they do come to pass. Jesus put this emotion in its proper little corner and set his disciples free from its bondage. So often did he tell his disciples not to fear that we might conclude that a big part of his purpose in walking the paths of this world was to set us free from fear. Sprinkled throughout his conversation are the expressions "Fear not," "Be not afraid." In that long and earnest talk with the disciples just before his crucifixion, he began with "Let not your heart be troubled"; then in the middle of it he repeated, "Let not your heart be troubled," and to reinforce it he added, ". . . neither let it be afraid." He followed this with a most important sentence, the significance of which we can so easily miss, "And now I have told you before it come to pass, that, when it is come to pass, ye might believe." He, of course, is speaking of his death and telling them that since they know it and are expecting it they will not be afraid and run away. The truth will make them free of terror. It will even make them more certain that he is God's Son and strengthen their belief. If these disciples were to fulfil their mission, they must master fear. Truth is the most valuable weapon given us to enable us to conquer the crippling fears.

For centuries the eclipse of the sun struck terror into the people of the earth, and it does to this day among the uncivilized, primitive tribes. When we learned the truth about this darkened sun, we no longer feared. We were set free.

113

Yellow fever epidemics once made people leave their homes and possessions and flee in panic. We learned the truth about yellow fever, and the fear of the epidemic was forgotten. We were set free.

I watched a camel caravan in Palestine. Each camel had a blue bead tied around its neck. Every Arab baby wore a blue bead for the same purpose—to keep away the evil spirit. The truth would set them free.

For many years I fished in the Gulf Stream off the Florida coast in a twenty-eight-foot boat. The one thing I feared most was a squall. Many, many times the day's fishing was spoiled because this danger made us run for protection into harbor or between two islands. Then one day I took an old sea captain along as a guest. When a "squall" loomed up black and ugly, I told him that we had better call it a day and get inside the jetties. He lifted his wrinkled, bronzed face, glanced at the storm, and remarked, "Nothing to be afraid of—there's no wind in that cloud." Astonished, I asked, "How do you know?" "Look at the edges. If there was any wind in it, they would be frayed and ragged." The cloud spread over us and released its refreshing shower. There was no wind, and I wondered how many times the fear of something that was harmless had spoiled a day for me. Truth would have set me free.

Dr. Clarence Macartney illustrated this lesson with an interesting personal experience. "When I was a boy, my father sent me on an errand late in the afternoon. If I hurried, I could possibly get back through the deep woods before dark. I trotted most of the way; nevertheless, when I got back to those deep woods, the sun was down, and the long, straight path was already gloomy and half lighted.

"I had gone only a little way when I saw a monster coming toward me—a great, burly monster that almost shut out the light of the path ahead. I stood stock-still. I couldn't make my feet go. I couldn't go backward; they just wouldn't move. I stood there trembling, and the tears came rolling down my cheeks. When the monster got a little closer, I saw it was a great big man, and I was still more afraid. I was too scared to cry out. I was paralyzed, so I just stood and waited. And then when he got almost to me, I saw it was my daddy. I went running and whimpering and told him what had happened. I learned a lesson; I learned a great lesson. Oftentimes the things that look like monsters and look like something that would kill us are the sweetest and loveliest things that ever come to us. They even bring us the choice blessings; they are the things that make us continually grateful and thankful."

Isn't that what Jesus was talking about? He said to these disciples: "Tomorrow they are going to crucify me; tomorrow they are going to nail me to a cross. But let not your heart be troubled. Don't think that is the worst thing that ever happened to you." He could have lifted the veil and said: "The time will come when you will take that old wooden cross the Roman soldier used and make it a symbol of glory and victory. There will be a time when you will stand up and sing that God loved us so that he gave his only begotten Son that whosoever believeth on him should not perish, but have everlasting life. The cross and the crucifixion and the resurrection will be the grandest things in your lives. I came to set you free. You shall know the truth, and when you know the truth about why I came, when you know the truth about what happened to me and that the grave couldn't hold me, you will shout and sing and preach. The resurrection and the glory of the resurrection will be celebrated across this wide world by millions and millions of people. When you know the truth, you will be free of fear."

115

The truth shall set you free from selfishness and indifference. We seem to be born selfish. One of the first words that we lisp is the word "mine." A little later we become self-centered; we want everything to revolve around us. We are entirely indifferent to the wishes of others. We want our way and go into a tantrum if we don't have it. If we are not corrected and disciplined, we naturally grow that way. It is no wonder that Jesus said, "Ye must be born again."

When we know him, we want to be like him. We want to have a part in his plans. We want to bear some fruit in his kingdom.

One of my fellow pastors wrote me this recently: "You'll enjoy this, so I am passing it on to you. I was in Houston, Texas, for the Baptist Student Union Convention, and we had about a thousand young people there. The Lamar Hotel was our headquarters. I came down to breakfast one morning and walked into the dining room that was filled with some of the finest Christian youth of America. I was happy to be a part of this. I sat down and listened to them gaily chatting. I listened to their wholesome conversation. It was on the highest level. It was good. When I went over to pay my check, the cashier was sitting down. She said: 'You can't pay your check. It's already been paid.' I asked, 'Who paid it?' 'I don't know. A gentleman came up to pay for his breakfast and asked me who these young people were. When I told him, he said: "I want to pay for their breakfasts. I want to pay for all of their breakfasts. I want to have a part in this." I said, "Well, you'll have to go up and see the manager." So, I say to you that I don't know who he is. You'll have to go up and talk to the manager.'"

My fellow pastor went up to see the manager. The manager smilingly said: "Yes, he's Mister Blank, and when I asked him why he wanted to pay the check, he said: 'Listen, they were all around me, that bunch of students. When they came in, they bowed their heads silently in prayer, every one of them. I listened to their conversation. Not a word of profanity did I hear. They were exuberant, they were happy. There was no sad solemnity. They were living. I want a part in it. I want a part in what they are and what they are doing. Let me pay for the breakfast of every single one of them.' "

That is what Christ wants to do for us—set us free from the shackles of sin and fear and selfishness, push back the horizons, make life bigger and finer and more wonderful.

Our gracious Father, we would have a part in thy plans; so keep us so pure and good that our lives may adorn the gospel. Amen.

Judge not, that ye be not judged. For with what judgment ye judge, ye shall be judged: and with what measure ye mete, it shall be measured to you again. And why beholdest thou the mote that is in thy brother's eye, but considerest not the beam that is in thine own eye? Or how wilt thou say to thy brother, Let me pull out the mote out of thine eye; and, behold, a beam is in thine own eye? Thou hypocrite, first cast out the beam out of thine own eye; and then shalt thou see clearly to cast out the mote out of thy brother's eye.

MATTHEW 7:1–5

13

The Tiny Mote

There is a delightful touch of humor, even a tinkle of laughter, in the Master's words: "And why beholdest thou the mote that is in thy brother's eye, but considerest not the beam that is in thine own eye? Or how wilt thou say to thy brother, Let me pull out the mote out of thine eye; and, behold, a beam is in thine own eye? Thou hypocrite, first cast out the beam out of thine own eye; and then shalt thou see clearly to cast out the mote out of thy brother's eye." We think of Jesus too often as being sad. There is a difference between being sad and being serious. He's serious here. But that does not prevent him from using laughter.

Christ realized that laughter is a powerful medicine. "A merry heart doeth good like a medicine." It is also a most effective weapon. He is using it here as a weapon. He's trying to get his listeners to laugh something out—not out of court, but out of life. We all know how deep are the cuts and how red our faces become when someone laughs at us. Jesus is not laughing *at* anyone, but he's trying to make a deadly habit so ridiculous that we would laugh it out of our lives. In the argot he said, "Why do you try to get a speck out of your brother's eye when there's a plank in your own eye?"

119

What is this habit Jesus is holding up for our scorn? It is so plain. It is the habit of being hypercritical or, in just plain English words, of "faultfinding." It is the habit of looking for, searching for the little things that do not belong in the life of someone else. A mote could float on a sunbeam. You would never see it in someone's eye if you weren't looking for it with a magnifying glass. Here is one sin which I have never heard anyone confess. And I am pretty sure the reason is neither dishonesty nor a lack of frankness. The real reason is that in our lives this thing is so subtle and so hard to see. We can see it in other people, but to see it in ourselves is most difficult. If you doubt the presence of this dangerous and disastrous habit in your life, then examine yourself for one day. Now, you'll have to stop about every three hours and look back to see if in that time you audibly or in your mind have found fault with anyone. I hope it doesn't amaze, shock, and humiliate you like it did me when I tried it. Christ isn't talking about something that's over the heads of people and not down where they live. This is an all too prevalent sin, and it is so deadly.

I was watching the *March of Time* on television one day, with this verse very much in my mind, when I saw, first, East Germany under communism with its marching soldiers. The commentator said, "The armed forces of Germany walking in close formation with something of the swagger of the goose step look about the same to the rest of the world as they did under Hitler."

And then the scene changed, and it was West Germany under *our* control. A great crowd of people were listening to a speaker just before an election. The camera switched to another street. There came miles and miles of tanks, all armed and ready for action, and then long columns of marching women followed by marching men. Apparently, the man who was describing the picture suddenly realized the inconsistency of his first remark and said, "But all of these were out of sight when the election took place." It is so easy to see the faults of others. It is a different thing to see our own. It is so easy to recognize a "faultfinder" among our friends; it is so difficult to see the faultfinder in our own lives.

Christ isn't talking to the scribes and the Pharisees. Don't mix this up with the statement of Jesus when he told of some who "strain at a gnat and swallow a camel." He was talking to the scribes and the Pharisees then, but here he is talking to his followers. Why is this habit of faultfinding so dangerous? Why is it so deadly? I can think of two big reasons. We can't afford to overlook either one of them.

First, it can wreck your peace of mind and your physical life. I recently read of a most interesting and most enlightening experiment of Doctors Fink and Gibson. I think the world ought to read it. I think it ought to be put in pamphlet form and given away. There walked into their big psychiatric clinic one day a wealthy industrialist, prominent in civic affairs. He said to Dr. Fink: "I am so restless and so tense. I can't relax; I sleep badly. There is nothing physically the matter with me, nothing morally the matter with me. I want you to find something that will help relax me." Dr. Fink said, "Well, there have been a great many books written on it." He said: "I've read some of them, but who has time to practice all the things they advocate? Dr. Fink, can't you and your big clinic find some button I can press or some magic key that will relax me of the tension under which I live?"

Dr. Fink said: "It was a challenge. I wondered if we had overlooked something. I wondered if there *was* a magic key. Dr. Gibson and I called our whole staff together. After we

121

had talked for two hours, we decided that we'd go back over the case histories of the last two years and see if there was a common divisor; if there was one thing—a magic key—that people who suffered from tension had in common. We divided the case histories into what we called two great haystacks to hunt for a needle. One of these stacks had all the tension cases; one had no tension cases. Slowly there emerged, to our astonishment, one single common divisor, just one. There was one single fault, one trait, one habit which every person who lived under tension had that was not present in the other haystack. The magic key—we had it! It was being hypercritical. It was being a "faultfinder." I'm using his words—"being a faultfinder."

He said: "We were so astonished we sat for hours. Immediately we took a hundred people who were suffering from tension and told them the whole story and gave them a trial recipe for straightening out their lives. Seventy out of the hundred came out splendidly; another twenty-two admitted they hadn't tried. If there is one thing that ought to be preached from every pulpit in this world it is that Jesus said, 'Get the beam out of your own eye before you go hunting a mote in the eye of someone else.'" Dr. Fink didn't say it in those words, but that is what he said. Christ was sharpshooting when he spoke this sentence. Faultfinding is a trait of American people today that is wrecking more happiness than we realize. Of course, all tension doesn't come from this; but there was not a single case of tension in the files of these two great doctors that did not have this trait of faultfinding in it. Whether you open your mouth or not, if you look at other people and their actions and at their work and criticize them, you get the feeling that they are criticizing you too. You can't live under pressure like that. It is too severe.

122

Now, the other reason that this thing is so deadly is that it hurts everybody else. It hurts other people. You can't possibly criticize them without hurting them. Faultfinders have no friends. Friendships cease when faultfinding begins.

There was a man who worshiped in my church years ago, and when I stood at the door at the end of the service to shake hands with the people as they came out, I always drooped when I saw him coming. There was something wrong with every sermon or every service—something wrong with the choir, with the church, and with everything about it. There was always at least one thing wrong about every service. I have never talked to him—and I have talked to him literally hundreds of times, I think—without hearing some criticism. It is difficult to love anybody like that very much. Hypercriticism hurts. It hurts the other person; it hurts you.

We recently invited the chief of detectives of Miami, Mr. Tom Lipe, to be the speaker at our Brotherhood banquet. He took as his subject "Three C's" and began his address by saying that he had just finished Dale Carnegie's course on friendships. Among the many fine things that he learned was this important lesson: "If you want to keep friends and have people like you, there are three things you must never do. Each one of these things begins with a *c*. The first one is, 'Never complain'; the second, 'Never condemn'; and the last one, 'Never criticize.' " He enlarged on each one of these, but put the most emphasis on the last one. He said a very thoughtful thing: "Criticizing people will put you under a strain and tension. The simple reason is that you realize that the criticism may have reached their ears, and so when you meet them somewhere, you are afraid to be nice to them; you are almost afraid to talk to them. You wonder how much of what you said has been repeated to them. If you dare fellowship

123

with them in the presence of the one to whom you spoke the criticism, you know he will be thinking you are a hypocrite. You are caught between a pair of ugly pincers. It makes you ill at ease, and the tension mounts."

Then how can we conquer this habit? Is there a cure for it? If so, what is the cure? Jesus and Paul both had something to say regarding this truth. When Paul said, "Work out your own salvation," he was not talking about the salvation of the soul. He was talking about getting rid of some of the debris and some of the ugly habits in our lives and replacing them with service in the vineyard of the Lord. He knew the importance of mental habits, so he said, "If there be anything pure, anything of good report . . . think on these things." Deliberately put out of your minds the critical and condemning thoughts about others, and look for the good. Jesus told of a man who had put a demon out of his life and garnished the room and left it empty. He pointed out the danger of tossing all the unclean and unwholesome things out of life and not replacing them with beautiful habits. "Pray for them that despitefully use you." Do good to them that do evil.

There is a story that was good enough to be printed 100,000 times. The man who wrote it said that he was trying to get rid of some habits and some things that he had been doing which were inconsistent with the Christian life. So at a Sunday morning service in his church he rededicated his life. After a year he wrote a little pamphlet that read something like this: "I made up my mind I was going to put something beautiful in the place of the things that I had ceased doing. I decided that I would deliberately try to make some one person happy every day. One evening I realized I hadn't done my happiness turn. Then I thought of a man who was ill and had been confined to his home for about three years. I didn't

124

have time to go to see him, so I picked up my telephone and
called him. When he came to the phone, he was so excited
and astonished that his voice quavered as he said, 'Hello?
What do you want?' 'Oh,' I said, 'I just called up to tell you
that I was thinking about you and wanted to hear your voice.
I want to get over to see you before very long. I hope you aren't
suffering too much and that having to stay in the house isn't
too hard on you.' He was so delighted and surprised that it
was hard for him to speak at first. Then he quieted down, and
we had a nice long visit over the phone. A few days later I
met his wife, and she said: 'You know, he is still talking about
your telephone call. He had said two days before, "The
phone never rings for me." ' " Do you reckon the man who
made that call had any tension in his life that night as he
lived over the deeds of the day? After hearing what his
friend's wife had to say, don't you think there was a glow of
satisfaction in his heart?

"How beautiful upon the mountain are the feet of him
that bringeth good tidings." How much happier we would be
if we thought and said good things, kind things, to each other
instead of criticizing or condemning or complaining.

Forgive us, our Father, if we are guilty of this deadly, de-
structive sin. Help us not to ruin our influence as Christians
by doing this thing that carries with it such little satisfaction
to us and which can be so harmful to the lives of others.
We all find it hard, our Heavenly Father, to pray for them
that despitefully use us. We find it so easy to criticize and
condemn them. Grant that we shall not follow the line of
least resistance but rather live a life in which there is no
guile and in which the Spirit of Jesus manifests itself daily.
May we establish the beautiful habit of looking for some-
thing good in others and for something that we might do to
make others happy. We ask it all in Jesus' name. Amen.